التقوى

TAQWA

THE PATH TO SUCCESS

Muhammad ibn Salih al-Uthaymin

TAMYEEZ PUBLICATIONS
ISLAMIC BOOK PUBLICATIONS

ISBN Softcover	:	979-8-89238-203-8
ISBN Hardcover	:	979-8-87208-903-2
First Edition	:	Rabi' al-Thani 1445/October 2023
Translation	:	Abu Maryam Khaleel Abdur Razaaq
Editing, Typesetting & Cover Design	:	Aljadeed Design Co.
Subject	:	Purification of the Soul
Website	:	www.Tamyeezpubs.com
Email	:	info@Tamyeezpubs.com

بسم الله الرحمن الرحيم

In the Name of Allāh, The Most-Merciful (to His creation), the Ever-Merciful (to His believing servants).

المحتويات

Table of Contents

A BRIEF BIOGRAPHY OF THE AUTHOR 8

AT-TAQWĀ & ITS MEANING 15

Definition of at-Taqwā 16

Intention of at-Taqwā 19

Taqwā is Contingent on the Ability! 21

Allāh Commanded Us to Have His Taqwā and to Say a Statement That is Sadīd 25

THE BENEFITS & FRUITS OF AT-TAQWĀ 27

Allāh's Taqwā Removes Difficulty and Increases Provisions 28

Allāh Will Give You a Furqān! 31

Allāh Will Remove Your Sins 34

Seeking Forgiveness Becomes Easy! 36

EXPLANATION OF THE ḤADĪTHS THAT COMMAND WITH TAQWĀ OF ALLĀH 39

The First Ḥadīth 40

The Second Ḥadīth 44

The Third Ḥadīth 50
The Fourth Ḥadīth 57
The Fifth Ḥadīth 62
THE BENEFITS OF TAQWĀ FROM THE NOBLE QUR'ĀN 69
Taqwā of Allāh is the Best Provision the Servant Has for the Benefits of His Religion and Worldly Affairs 70
CONCLUSION 130

Transliteration Table

Consonants

ء	'	د	d	ض	ḍ	ك	k
ب	b	ذ	dh	ط	ṭ	ل	l
ت	t	ر	r	ظ	ẓ	م	m
ث	th	ز	z	ع	'	ن	n
ج	j	س	s	غ	gh	ه	h
ح	ḥ	ش	sh	ف	f	و	w
خ	kh	ص	ṣ	ق	q	ي	y

Vowels

Short	ـَ	a	ـِ	i	ـُ	u
Long	ـَا	ā	ـِي	ī	ـُو	ū
Diphthongs	ـَي	ay	ـَو	aw		

Arabic Glyphs & Their Meanings

صَلَّى ٱللَّهُ عَلَيْهِ وَسَلَّمَ May Allāh's praise & salutations be upon him	رَضِيَ ٱللَّهُ عَنْهُ May Allāh be pleased with him	رَضِيَ ٱللَّهُ عَنْهَا May Allāh be pleased with her
رَضِيَ ٱللَّهُ عَنْهُمْ May Allāh be pleased with them	سُبْحَانَهُ وَتَعَالَىٰ Glorified & Exalted is Allāh	عَزَّ وَجَلَّ (Allāh) the Mighty & Sublime
جَلَّ جَلَالُهُ (Allāh) His Majesty is Exalted	تَبَارَكَ وَتَعَالَىٰ (Allāh) the Blessed & Exalted	عَلَيْهِ ٱلسَّلَامُ Peace be upon Him
رَحِمَهُ ٱللَّهُ May Allāh have mercy on him	رَحِمَهُمُ ٱللَّهُ May Allāh have mercy upon them	حَفِظَهُ اللهُ May Allāh preserve him

A BRIEF BIOGRAPHY OF THE AUTHOR

Shaykh Al-ʿAllāmah Muḥammad bin Sālih Al-ʿUthaymīn رَحِمَهُ ٱللَّهُ

HIS NAME, BIRTH AND LINEAGE

He was, Al-ʿAllāmah Al-Faqīh Abū Abdullah Muḥammad Ibn Sālih Ibn Muḥammad Ibn Al-ʿUthaymīn At-Tamīmī An-Najdī. Shaykh ʿUthaymīn, as he was most known, was born in the city of Unayzah, Qaseem Region, Saudi Arabia, on 27th Ramadhan 1347H in a famous religious family.

HIS EDUCATION

He received his education from many renowned scholars such as: Shaykh ʿAbdur-Rahmaan Ibn Naasir As-Sa'di (1307H – 1376H), Shaykh Muhammad Ameen Ash-Shanqeeti (1325H – 1393H), and Shaykh Abdul-Azeez Ibn Baz (1330H – 1420H), along with many more.

When he entered into teaching, a great number of students from inside and outside Saudi Arabia benefited from him. He had his own unique style of interpretation and explanation of religious points. He was from among those scholars who served Islaam without any type of religious prejudice and kept themselves away from the limitations of blind-following. He was distinguished in his great exertion of effort in religious matters and analogical deductions which clearly prove the religious understanding he possessed, and the correct usage of the principles of religion, he adopted.

Along with Shaykh Nasiruddin Albaani (d.1420H), Shaykh Abdul-Azeez Ibn Baz (d.1420H), and Shaykh Muqbil Ibn Haadi Al-Waadi'i (d.1422H), are the era of 1400H top Ahlus Sunnah scholars so far, although many more deserve to be mentioned in the strive for this Deen of Islam also, such as Shaykh Abdullah Ibn Abdur-Rahman Al-Jibreen, Shaykh Saeed Ibn Ali Ibn Wahf Al-Qahtaani, Shaykh Dr. Saleh Ibn Fawzan Ibn Abdullah Al-Fawzan, Shaykh Muhammad Ibn Jameel Zainoo, Shaykh Muhammad Saleh Al-Munajjid, Shaykh Saifur-Rahman Mubarakpooree, among others.

In giving religious verdicts, like Shaykh Ibn Baaz, Shaykh 'Uthaymīn Fataawa (i.e, rulings/verdicts) are based on the Manhaj of Ahlus Sunnah wal Jamaa'ah which is evidenced from Qur'aan and Sunnah. He has about fifty compilations to his credit. Recently before his death, he was teaching religious Fundamentals at the Sharee'ah Faculty of Imam Muhammad Ibn Sa'ud Islamic University, Qaseem Branch. He was also a member of the Senior Scholars Committee of the Kingdom, and was the Imaam and Khateeb of the big Mosque of Unayzah city.

HIS POSITIONS

- Former member of the Council of Senior Scholars of Saudi Arabia from 1407 until his death.
- Former member of the Scholastic Council of the Muhammad Ibn

Sa'ood Islaamic University.

- Former member of the council of the Sharee'ah and Usool ad Deen faculty as well as president of the 'Aqeedah branch of the Muhammad Ibn Sa'ood Islaamic University branch in Qaseem.
- Former member of the Council of Education and Enlightenment during the Hajj season from 1392 until his death.
- Former president of the non-profit Memorization of the Noble Quraan Society in 'Unayzah from 1405 until his death.

AMONG HIS WELL-KNOWN WORKS IN DA'WAH

- Tafsir Ayatul Kursi.
- Sharh Riyadh Saleheen.
- Kitab ul Ilm.
- Sharh Usool Thalaathah.
- Fataawa Arkan Islam.
- Majmoo' Fataawa on many topics of Islamic Aqeedah and Fiqh.
- A collection of Fataawa and Treatise.
- Tafseer Al Qur'aan Al Kareem.
- Gatherings in the Month of Ramadaan.
- Al Qawl Al Mufeed 'ala Kitaab At Tawheed.
- Ash Sharh Al-Mumti' Ala Zaadil Mustaqni'.
- The Book of Knowledge [Translated].
- Taqreeb At Tadmooriyyah.

- Exemplary Foundations Concerning the Beautiful Names and Attributes of Allaah [Translated].
- Explanation of Al Arba'een An Nawawiyyah [Translated].
- Fath Rab Al Bariyyah.
- Mukhtasar Ma'naa Al Labeeb.
- Explanation of Al 'Aqeedah Al Waasityyah [Translated].
- Explanation of Lum'at Al 'Itiqaad.
- Manaasik Al Hajj Wal 'Umrah.
- Al Usool min 'Ilm Al Usool.
- Tasheel Al Faraa'id.
- Mustalah Al Hadeeth.
- The Description of the Prophets Hajj.
- Being Balanced in Da'wah.
- Treatise on Hijaab [Translated].
- Al Manhaj li Mureed Al 'Umrah Wal Hajj.
- The Rulings of Slaughtering.
- 48 Questions on Fasting [Translated].
- The Provisions of the Caller to Allaah.
- Difference of Opinion Amongst the Scholars and its Causes [Translated].
- Debts.
- 60 Questions of the Rulings of Menses.

- Chapters on Fasting, Taraweeh and Zakaah [Translated]
- Minhaaj Ahlus Sunnah wal Jamaa'ah.
- Wiping Over the Khufs.
- The Ruling of one who abandons the Prayer.
- Allaah's Names and Attributes.
- 'Aqeedat Ahlus Sunnah wal Jamaa'ah.
- A Collection of Questions related to the Family.
- Normal Blood concerning Women.
- Errors some Hujjaaj fall Into.
- Zakaat Al Hulee.
- Sujood As Sahw.
- Divine Decree.
- How does a Muslim perform Hajj and 'Umrah.
- A Summary of Fiqh Al Faraa'id.
- Buying and Selling Gold.
- The Fundamentals of Tafseer.
- The Valuable Remembrance.
- Prohibited Statements.
- Marriage [Translated].
- Description of the Prophets Prayer.
- Essential Rights that the Fitrah Calls To.

- Co-operation between the Du'aat and its Effect on the Community.
- The Prescribed Times of Prayer.
- The Explanation of the D'ua of Qunoot Al Witr.
- From the Problems of the Youth.
- How an Ill Person Purifies Himself.
- Explanation of Saheeh Al Bukhaaree.
- Explanation of Riyaad As Saaliheen.
- Explanation of Buloogh Al Maraam.
- Explanation of Al 'Aqeedah Al Waasitiyyah.
- Explanation of Al Ajroomiyyah.
- Explanation of Lum'at Al 'Itiqaad.
- Explanation of Al Arba'een An Nawawiyyah.
- Explanation of Al Bayqooniyyah.
- Explanation of The Three Fundamental Principles.
- Explanation of Kashf Ash Shubuhaat.
- Explanation of Al 'Aqeedah As Safareeniyyah.
- Explanation of Nukhbat Al Fikr.
- Explanation of Nadhm Al Waraqaat.
- Explanation of 'Umdat Al Ahkaam.
- An Introduction to the Principles of Tafseer.

- Explanation of Alfeeyat Ibn Maalik.
- Explanation of Kitaab At Tawheed.
- Explanation of Al Fataawa Al Hamawiyyah.

HIS CHARACTER

Shaykh 'Uthaymīn was famous for his simplicity, modesty, along with exceptional mannerisms towards all those he encountered, as well as his exceptional mannerisms in approach to topics free of dogmatic arguments. He is among the pre-eminent scholars of the era after 1400H.

HIS DEATH

Shaykh 'Uthaymīn passed away on Wednesday 15th Shawwal, 1421H/10th January 2001 C.E. He was buried in Makkah along with his peers among the scholars Shaykh Ibn Baz, while Shaykh Muqbil Ibn Haadi Al-Waadi'i. He was 74 years of age. May Allaah (subhaanahu wa ta'aala) have Mercy upon his soul, aameen.

SECTION ONE

At-Taqwā & its Meaning

Definition of at-Taqwā

Taqwā is a word taken from *Wiqāyah*, which means to take shelter. It is that an individual takes protection from Allāh's punishment. Fulfilling Allāh's commands and staying distant from His prohibitions is what shelters you from His punishment. Therefore, hold fast to Allāh's commands and abandon what He has forbidden.

Know, at times, *Taqwā* is connected to the word *Birr*. Thus, it is said *Birr* and *Taqwā*, as is in the Statement of Allāh (سُبۡحَانَهُۥ وَتَعَالَىٰ):

﴿وَتَعَاوَنُوا۟ عَلَى ٱلۡبِرِّ وَٱلتَّقۡوَىٰ﴾

> **"And aid you one another in *al-Birr* and *at-Taqwā*."**
> [Sūrah al-Mā'idah 5:2]

Other times, it is mentioned alone. If it is connected to *Birr*, *Birr* takes the meaning of fulfilling the commands, and *Taqwā* means to leave off the prohibitions. If it is mentioned alone, the word *Taqwā* contains both definitions, fulfilling the commandments and staying distant from the prohibitions.

Allāh (سُبۡحَانَهُۥ وَتَعَالَىٰ) has mentioned in his book that the *Jannah* (Paradise) has been prepared for the *Muttaqīn* (those who possess *Taqwā*). Therefore, the people of *Taqwā* are the people of the *Jannah* (Paradise). May Allāh make us from them. For that reason, it is obligatory upon the people to have the *Taqwā* of Allāh (سُبۡحَانَهُۥ وَتَعَالَىٰ) by fulfilling His commands, seeking His reward and safety from His punishment. After that, the author mentioned several verses. He said:

﴿يَٰٓأَيُّهَا ٱلَّذِينَ ءَامَنُواْ ٱتَّقُواْ ٱللَّهَ حَقَّ تُقَاتِهِۦ﴾

> **"O you who believe! Fear Allāh as he ought to be feared."** [Sūrah āl-'Imrān 3:102]

And He (سُبۡحَانَهُۥ وَتَعَالَىٰ) also said:

﴿فَٱتَّقُواْ ٱللَّهَ مَا ٱسۡتَطَعۡتُمۡ﴾

> **"And fear Allāh as much as you are able."** [Sūrah at-Taghābun 64:16]

This verse clarifies the intent of the first one.

Allāh (سُبۡحَانَهُۥ وَتَعَالَىٰ) also said:

﴿يَٰٓأَيُّهَا ٱلَّذِينَ ءَامَنُواْ ٱتَّقُواْ ٱللَّهَ وَقُولُواْ قَوۡلٗا سَدِيدٗا ٧٠﴾

> **"O you who believe! Fear Allāh and say a statement that**

is *Sadīd* (correct and in its place).” [Sūrah al-Aḥzāb 33:70]

The verses that command with *Taqwā* are many and known. Allāh (سُبْحَانَهُ وَتَعَالَىٰ) said:

﴿وَمَن يَتَّقِ ٱللَّهَ يَجْعَل لَّهُۥ مَخْرَجًا ۝٢ وَيَرْزُقْهُ مِنْ حَيْثُ لَا يَحْتَسِبُ﴾

“And whoever has the *Taqwā* of Allāh, He will make a way out for him from every difficulty and provide for him from where he never anticipated.” [Sūrah at-Ṭalāq 65:2-3]

He (سُبْحَانَهُ وَتَعَالَىٰ) also said:

﴿إِن تَتَّقُوا۟ ٱللَّهَ يَجْعَل لَّكُمْ فُرْقَانًا وَيُكَفِّرْ عَنكُمْ سَيِّـَٔاتِكُمْ وَيَغْفِرْ لَكُمْ ۗ وَٱللَّهُ ذُو ٱلْفَضْلِ ٱلْعَظِيمِ ۝٢٩﴾

“If you fear Allāh, He will give you a *Furqān* (a criterion to judge between truth and falsehood), remove for you your sins, and forgive you, and Allāh is the Possessor of great bounty.” [Sūrah al-Anfāl 8:29]

The verses in this area are numerous and known.

Intention of at-Taqwā

His statement:

﴿يَٰٓأَيُّهَا ٱلَّذِينَ ءَامَنُوا۟ ٱتَّقُوا۟ ٱللَّهَ حَقَّ تُقَاتِهِۦ﴾

> **"O you who believe! Fear Allāh as he ought to be feared."** [Sūrah āl-ʿImrān 3:102]

Here, he is directing the command to the believers because the *Īmān* of the believer carries him to having the *Taqwā* of Allāh.

His statement:

﴿يَٰٓأَيُّهَا ٱلَّذِينَ ءَامَنُوا۟ ٱتَّقُوا۟ ٱللَّهَ حَقَّ تُقَاتِهِۦ﴾

> **"Fear Allāh as he ought to be feared."** [Sūrah āl-ʿImrān 3:102]

The author (رَحِمَهُ ٱللَّهُ) has followed this verse with another, explaining the actual reality of *Taqwā*:

﴿فَٱتَّقُوا۟ ٱللَّهَ مَا ٱسْتَطَعْتُمْ﴾

> **"Fear Allāh as much as you are able."** [Sūrah at-Taghābun 64:16]

This means you fear Allāh as much as possible because Allāh does not burden a person beyond his scope.

﴿فَٱتَّقُوا۟ ٱللَّهَ مَا ٱسْتَطَعْتُمْ﴾

> **"Fear Allāh as much as you are able."** [Sūrah at-Taghābun 64:16]

Taqwā is Contingent on the Ability!

Being lax about Allāh's *Taqwā* is not the intent; the only purpose here is an incitement to *Taqwā*, according to one's ability. This means spare no effort in Allāh's *Taqwā*; however, Allāh does not burden a person beyond his ability in anything, just as Allāh (سُبْحَانَهُ وَتَعَالَىٰ) has said:

﴿لَا يُكَلِّفُ ٱللَّهُ نَفْسًا إِلَّا وُسْعَهَا﴾

> **"Allāh burdens not a person beyond his scope."** [Sūrah al-Baqarah 2:286]

The benefit we take from his statement:

﴿فَٱتَّقُوا۟ ٱللَّهَ مَا ٱسْتَطَعْتُمْ﴾

> **"Fear Allāh as much as you are able."** [Sūrah at-Taghābun 64:16]

If an individual cannot fulfill one of Allāh's commands completely, he must perform it according to his capacity level. The statement of the Prophet (ﷺ) to Imrān bin Husain is from that:

«صَلِّ قَائِمًا فَإِنْ لَمْ تَسْتَطِعْ فَقَاعِدًا فَإِنْ لَمْ تَسْتَطِعْ فَعَلَى جَنْبٍ»

> **"Pray standing; if you are not able, then sitting; if you are not able, then on your side."**

Thus, the Prophet (ﷺ) arranged the *Salāh* according to the ability, in as much that he prays standing; if he is not able, then sitting; if he is not able, then on his side. The remaining commands are also similar. An example is fasting. If someone is not able to fast in the month of *Ramadān*, he delays it, as Allāh said:

﴿وَمَن كَانَ مَرِيضًا أَوْ عَلَىٰ سَفَرٍ فَعِدَّةٌ مِّنْ أَيَّامٍ أُخَرَ﴾

> **"Whoever is ill or on a journey, then an equal Benefit of other days."** [Sūrah al-Baqarah 2:185]

Likewise, is the *Ḥajj* (Pilgrimage to Mecca) as Allāh said:

﴿وَلِلَّهِ عَلَى ٱلنَّاسِ حِجُّ ٱلْبَيْتِ﴾

> **"For Allāh upon the people is to make *Ḥajj* (Pilgrimage) to the House."** [Sūrah āl-ʿImrān 3:97]

This is for the one who can find a way to get there. Therefore, if you are not able to reach the House in Mecca, the *Ḥajj* is not upon you;

however, if you are able, by way of your wealth, without the physical ability, it is obligatory upon you to establish someone to perform *Ḥajj* and *'Umrah* on your behalf.

The point: *Taqwā*, like other actions, is contingent on the ability. Thus, if one cannot conduct something of Allāh's commands, he turns to what he is able. Whoever is compelled to do something from Allāh's prohibitions, it is permissible for him to take from that (fundamentally impermissible) thing to repel the necessity. This is due to the statement of Allāh (سُبْحَانَهُ وَتَعَالَىٰ):

﴿وَقَدْ فَصَّلَ لَكُم مَّا حَرَّمَ عَلَيْكُمْ إِلَّا مَا ٱضْطُرِرْتُمْ إِلَيْهِ﴾

> **"He has explained in detail what He has forbidden you, except that to which you are compelled."** [Sūrah al-An'ām 6:119]

This reaches the extent that even if a man were compelled to eat the meat of a dead animal, swine, donkey meat, and so forth of the prohibitions, it is permissible for him to eat from it what will remove his dire need. This is the *Taqwā* of Allāh, to fulfill the commands as much as possible and stay distant from the prohibitions as much as possible.

The Statement of Allāh (سُبْحَانَهُ وَتَعَالَىٰ):

﴿يَـٰٓأَيُّهَا ٱلَّذِينَ ءَامَنُوا۟ ٱتَّقُوا۟ ٱللَّهَ وَقُولُوا۟ قَوْلًا سَدِيدًا ﴿٧٠﴾﴾

> **"O you who believe! Fear Allāh and say a statement that is *Sadīd* (correct and in its place)."** [Sūrah al-Aḥzāb 33:70]

Thus, Allāh (سُبْحَانَهُ وَتَعَالَىٰ) commanded us with two matters in this verse. He commanded us to have His *Taqwā* and to say a statement that is *Sadīd*, meaning: that which is correct.

Allāh Commanded Us to Have His Taqwā and to Say a Statement That is Sadīd

Speech regarding *Taqwā* has already preceded; it is fulfilling Allāh's commands and being distant from His prohibitions. As for a statement that is *Sadīd*, it is a statement that is correct. This contains every word that has good, whether from the remembrance of Allāh, seeking knowledge, ordering with what is good and forbidding from what is evil, from good speech that attracts the people's love and so on. The statement of the Prophet (ﷺ) brings it together:

« مَنْ كَانَ يُؤْمِنُ بِاللَّهِ وَالْيَوْمِ الْآخِرِ فَلْيَقُلْ خَيْرًا أَوْ لِيَصْمُتْ »

> **"Whoever believes in Allāh and the Last Day, let him say what is good or remain silent."**

Its opposite is a statement that is not *Sadīd*; it is a statement that is not correct; instead, it is a mistake, whether in its subject matter or its place. As for its subject matter, it is despicable speech; it contains abuse and revilement, backbiting, tale-carrying and what resembles that. In its place means that the statement within itself is good; however, it is said in an area that is not good because every place has a statement. Therefore, if you utter a word that within itself is not evil; however, it is a cause for evil to occur if you were to say it in this place, you should not say it because this is a statement that is not *Sadīd*, even if it is not impermissible in its essence.

Example: let's presume an individual has seen another committing an evil act, and he forbade him from this evil; however, he forbade him from it in a setting that is not proper for him to say anything, or he uttered it to him in a rude manner, or what resembles that, this statement of his is not *Sadīd*.

Thus, if an individual were to have the *Taqwā* of his Lord and say a statement that is *Sadīd*, two benefits would occur; Allāh says He will rectify your actions and forgive your sins. Thus, through *Taqwā* and a *Sadīd* word is correcting deeds and the forgiveness of sins.

It becomes known from this verse that whoever does not have Allāh's *Taqwā* nor speak a *Sadīd* statement, it is only befitting that Allāh does not rectify his actions nor forgive his sins.

Also, there is an incitement within this to have the *Taqwā* of Allāh, along with a clarification of its benefits.

SECTION TWO

The Benefits & Fruits of at-Taqwā

Allāh's Taqwā Removes Difficulty and Increases Provisions

Allāh (سُبْحَانَهُ وَتَعَالَىٰ) said in the fourth verse that the author (رَحِمَهُ ٱللَّهُ) mentioned:

﴿وَمَن يَتَّقِ ٱللَّهَ يَجْعَل لَّهُۥ مَخْرَجًا ۝٢ وَيَرْزُقْهُ مِنْ حَيْثُ لَا يَحْتَسِبُ﴾

> **"Whoever fears Allāh, He will make a way out for him from every difficulty and provide for him from where he never anticipated."** [Sūrah at-Ṭalāq 65:2-3]

Therefore, he has Allāh's *Taqwā* by doing what Allāh commanded and leaving off what he forbade. Allāh will make a way out for him from every difficulty and every constraint. Hence, anytime something becomes constrained for him while he is having the *Taqwā* of Allāh (سُبْحَانَهُ وَتَعَالَىٰ), He will make a way out for him, whether that be in his living, wealth, children, society, etc. Whenever you have the *Taqwā* of Allāh, rest assured that Allāh will soon provide a way out for you from every constraint. Trust that! Because it is the statement of the One Who says about something: "Be," and it is, and He said that whoever has His *Taqwā*, He will make a way out for him from every difficulty.

How abundant has it been! Those who had Allāh's *Taqwā* and He made a way out for them from their difficulty.

From that is the story of the three upon whom the cave enclosed; a boulder descended upon its opening and locked them in. They desired to move it but were incapable of doing so. Each of them implored Allāh through a righteous action they did for Allāh (سُبْحَانَهُ وَتَعَالَىٰ).

Thereupon, Allāh (سُبْحَانَهُ وَتَعَالَىٰ) created an opening for them, the boulder was removed, and He provided a way out for them. Examples of this are numerous.

The Statement of Allāh:

﴿وَيَرْزُقْهُ مِنْ حَيْثُ لَا يَحْتَسِبُ﴾

> **"And provide for him from where he never anticipated."**
> [Sūrah at-Ṭalāq 65:3]

Another great benefit is that Allāh provides for you from where you never expected.

For example, were we to assume that a man was to acquire wealth in an impermissible way, like deception, usury, or what resembles that, and somebody advised him regarding this; thus, he left it off for Allāh. Allāh will surely soon give him a way out of his difficulty and provide for him where he never anticipated. However, do not hasten and think that if the matter is delayed, it will not occur; perhaps Allāh is examining His servant and is delaying the reward to test him. Will he return to the sin or not? So, for example, had you dealt in usury and one were to come and admonish you and you were to leave that off; however, you were to remain a month or two and have not seen any profits or gains, do not despair and do not say: "Where are the provisions from where I do not anticipate?" Instead, wait and trust Allāh's promise; believe in Him, and you will discover it. Do not be hasty.

There has come, for this reason, in the *Ḥadīth* that:

« يُسْتَجَابُ لِأَحَدِكُمْ مَا لَمْ يَعْجَلْ »

The *Du'ā'* (supplication) of each of you is answered when you supplicate if you don't rush. It was said: "How does he rush O Messenger of Allāh?" He responded:

« يَقُولُ: دَعَوْتُ فَلَمْ يُسْتَجَبْ لِي »

"He says: 'I supplicated, and it was not answered for me.'"

Be patient and leave off what Allāh has forbidden and wait for the ease and provisions from where you do not expect.

Allāh Will Give You a Furqān!

The fifth verse is the Statement of Allāh (سُبْحَانَهُ وَتَعَالَى):

﴿إِن تَتَّقُواْ ٱللَّهَ يَجۡعَل لَّكُمۡ فُرۡقَانٗا وَيُكَفِّرۡ عَنكُمۡ سَيِّـَٔاتِكُمۡ
وَيَغۡفِرۡ لَكُمۡۗ وَٱللَّهُ ذُو ٱلۡفَضۡلِ ٱلۡعَظِيمِ ٢٩﴾

> **"If you fear Allāh, He will give you a *Furqān* (criterion to judge between truth and falsehood), remove your sins, and forgive you. And Allāh is the Possessor of Great Bounty."** [Sūrah al-Anfāl 8:29]

This has three significant benefits: the first benefit is that He will give you a *Furqān* (criterion to judge between truth and falsehood). Meaning: He will provide you with that which will enable you to distinguish between truth and falsehood and between what produces harm and benefit. Knowledge goes into this. In as much that Allāh will open for the people, various sciences that He does not open for others. Indeed, *Taqwā* produces an increase in guidance, knowledge, and memorization. It has been mentioned, for this reason, about Imām ash-Shāfiʿī

(رَحِمَهُ ٱللَّهُ) that he said: "I complained to Wakʿī of my poor memory. He directed me to leave from sins. He said to know that knowledge is a light, and the light of Allāh is not given to a sinner."

There is no doubt that whenever someone is given an increase in knowledge, his *Furqān* of judging between truth and falsehood and what brings benefit and harm also increases. Likewise, what Allāh opens for one of understanding is also from this because *Taqwā* is a reason for solid understanding and increased knowledge. Thus, you may come across two individuals memorizing a verse from the Book of Allāh, and one of the two may extract, for example, three rulings from that verse while the other can extract five, ten, or even more than this, according to what Allāh has given him of understanding. Hence, *Taqwā* is a reason for increased understanding.

Acumen is likewise from this. Allāh grants the one who has *Taqwā* acumen, with which he can distinguish between the people. By merely seeing someone, he knows whether he is a liar or truthful, whether he is righteous or wicked, to the point that he may be able to judge somebody while never associating closely with him nor knowing anything about him. This is due to what Allāh has given him of acumen. Also, what goes into this is the Miracles given to the *Muttaqīn* (those embellished with *Taqwā*). These miracles are only offered to them.

Of that is what occurred to many of the Companions (رَضِيَ ٱللَّهُ عَنْهُمْ) and the *Tābiʿīn* (those who met the Companions and believed in the message of Muḥammad (صَلَّى ٱللَّهُ عَلَيْهِ وَسَلَّمَ) and died upon that belief).

One day, ʿUmar bin al-Khaṭṭāb (رَضِيَ ٱللَّهُ عَنْهُ) was on the *minbar* in Medina. The people heard him say amid the *Khutbah* (sermon): "O Sāriyah! The mountain!"

Those whom he was addressing became astonished. How does he say this speech in the middle of the *Khutbah*?

At that juncture, Allāh (سُبْحَانَهُ وَتَعَالَى) had revealed to him the affair of a military detachment in Iraq. The name of their commander was Sāriyah bin Zanayn. The enemy surrounded them, and Allāh thus revealed to ʿUmar the matter of this military detachment. It was as though he witnessed it through his own eyes.

He said to this commander: O Sāriyah! The mountain! Meaning: fortify your position by the mountain. Sāriyah heard him while he was in Iraq. Thereupon, he took shelter by the mountain. This is from *Taqwā*.

All the miracles for Allāh's allies are a reward for them because of their *Taqwā* for Allāh (سُبْحَانَهُ وَتَعَالَى).

The important thing here is that from the effects of *Taqwā* is that Allāh (سُبْحَانَهُ وَتَعَالَى) gives the *Muttaqīn* (those embellished with *Taqwā*) a *Furqān* (criterion to judge) for them to distinguish, by way of it, between the truth and falsehood, the righteous and the wicked, and many things that only occur for the *Muttaqī* (singular for *Muttaqīn*).

Allāh Will Remove Your Sins

The second benefit: He will remove your sins. The removal of sins occurs through righteous actions. Righteous actions remove evil deeds, as the Prophet (ﷺ) said:

«الصَّلَوَاتُ الْخَمْسُ وَالْجُمْعَةُ إِلَى الْجُمْعَةِ وَرَمَضَانُ إِلَى رَمَضَانَ مُكَفِّرَاتٌ لِمَا بَيْنَهُنَّ مَا اجْتُنِبَتِ الْكَبَائِرُ»

"The five prayers, Jumu'ah to the next Jumu'ah, and Ramadān to the next Ramadān, remove the sins of what is between them as long as the major sins are avoided."

The Prophet (ﷺ) also said:

«الْعُمْرَةُ إِلَى الْعُمْرَةِ كَفَّارَةٌ لِمَا بَيْنَهُمَا»

"Umrah to the next 'Umrah removes what is between the two of them."

Therefore, the removal of sins occurs by way of righteous actions. This means that if someone were to have the *Taqwā* of Allāh, Allāh would make it easy for him to do virtuous actions with which Allāh will remove his sins.

Seeking Forgiveness Becomes Easy!

The third benefit is the Statement of Allāh (سُبْحَانَهُ وَتَعَالَىٰ):

﴿وَيَغْفِرْ لَكُمْ﴾

"And He will forgive you." [Sūrah al-Anfāl 8:29]

In as much that He will make it easy for you to seek forgiveness and repent. Indeed, making it easy for the servant to seek forgiveness and repent is from the blessings of Allāh upon him.

It is a test for the servant to believe that the sins he is committing are not sins. Therefore, he continues perpetrating them, and Allāh's refuge is sought.

This is just as Allāh (سُبْحَانَهُ وَتَعَالَىٰ) said:

﴿قُلْ هَلْ نُنَبِّئُكُم بِٱلْأَخْسَرِينَ أَعْمَٰلًا ﴿١٠٣﴾ ٱلَّذِينَ ضَلَّ سَعْيُهُمْ فِى ٱلْحَيَوٰةِ ٱلدُّنْيَا
وَهُمْ يَحْسَبُونَ أَنَّهُمْ يُحْسِنُونَ صُنْعًا ﴿١٠٤﴾﴾

"Say, [O Muḥammad (صَلَّىٱللَّهُعَلَيْهِوَسَلَّمَ)]: 'Shall we inform you of the greatest losers as to their deeds? They are those whose effort is lost in the worldly life while they think they are doing well in their work.'" [Sūrah al-Kahf 18:103-104]

Many people do not refrain from committing sins because they have been beautified for them, and Allāh's refuge is sought.

Thus, the servant becomes habituated to them, and these sins become difficult for him to extricate from. However, if he were to have the *Taqwā* of Allāh (سُبْحَانَهُوَتَعَالَىٰ), Allāh would make it easy for him to refrain from sins to forgive him, and perhaps, Allāh would forgive him because of his *Taqwā*.

His *Taqwā* would remove his sins, just as had occurred for the people of *Badr* (رَضِيَٱللَّهُعَنْهُمْ). Indeed, Allāh has informed the people of Badr:

"Do as you wish, verily, I have forgiven you."

Therefore, the sins they committed are forgiven because of what occurred to them in the Battle of Badr of great reward.

His Statement:

﴿وَٱللَّهُ ذُو ٱلْفَضْلِ ٱلْعَظِيمِ ﴿٢٩﴾﴾

> **"And Allāh is the Possessor of Great Bounty."** [Sūrah al-Anfāl 8:29]

Meaning: The likes of which nothing is equivalent. Since this description characterizes Allāh, request the bounty from Him. That is by way of having His *Taqwā* and returning to Him. And Allāh knows best.

SECTION THREE

Explanation of the Ḥadīths that Command with Taqwā of Allāh

The First Ḥadīth

«عَنْ أَبِي هُرَيْــرَةَ رَضِيَ اللَّهُ عَنْهُ قِيلَ يَا رَسُــولَ اللَّهِ، مَنْ أَكْرَمُ النَّاسِ؟ قَالَ أَتْقَاهُمْ فَقَالُوا لَيْسَ عَنْ هَذَا نَسْــأَلُكَ قَالَ فَيُوسُــفُ نَبِيُّ اللَّهِ ابْنُ نَبِيِّ اللَّهِ ابْنِ نَبِيِّ اللَّهِ ابْنِ خَلِيــلِ اللَّهِ قَالُوا لَيْسَ عَنْ هَذَا نَسْأَلُكَ قَالَ فَعَنْ مَعَادِنِ الْعَرَبِ تَسْأَلُونِ؟ خِيَارُهُمْ فِي الْجَاهِلِيَّةِ خِيَارُهُمْ فِي الْإِسْلَامِ إِذَا فَقُهُوا»

On the authority of Abu Huraira (رَضِيَ اللَّهُ عَنْهُ), he said:

> **"It was asked: 'O Messenger of Allāh! Who is the noblest of people?' He responded: 'Those who have the most Taqwā from them.' They said: 'This is not what we are asking you about.' He responded: 'Then Yūsuf, the Prophet of Allāh, the son of the Prophet of Allāh, the son of the Prophet of Allāh, the son of the Khalīl (the most intimate friend) of Allāh.' They said: 'This is not what we are asking you about.' Thereupon, he responded: 'Is it the descendants of the Arab that you are asking me about? The best of them**

> **in the pre-Islāmic days of ignorance is the best of them in Islām if they have understanding.'**

EXPLANATION

His statement: **"If they have understanding"** means that they know the rulings of the legislation. His response to their question: "Who is the noblest of the people?" ***"Those who have the most Taqwā from them."*** This means that the noblest of people are those who have the most *Taqwā* amongst them.

This answer is in complete conformity to the statement of Allāh (سُبْحَانَهُ وَتَعَالَىٰ):

﴿إِنَّ أَكْرَمَكُمْ عِندَ ٱللَّهِ أَتْقَىٰكُمْ﴾

> **"Verily, the noblest of you with Allāh are those who have the most *Taqwā*."** [Sūrah al-Ḥujurāt 49:13]

Therefore, Allāh (سُبْحَانَهُ وَتَعَالَىٰ) does not look to the people by their lineage, calculation, wealth, or beauty; He only looks to their actions. Thus, the noblest of them with Him are those who have the most *Taqwā*. For this reason, Allāh provides the people of *Taqwā* with the supplies He gives them of apparent and hidden miracles because they are the noblest of creation with Him.

There is an incitement within this to have Allāh's *Taqwā* (سُبْحَانَهُ وَتَعَالَىٰ). Whenever the people have the most *Taqwā*, they are the noblest of them with Him. However, the companions did not intend the most dignified of people with Allāh.

They said: "This is not what we are asking you about." Then he mentioned to them that the noblest of creation is Yūsuf, the son of the Prophet of Allāh, the son of the Prophet of Allāh, the son of the *Khalīl* of Allāh (i.e. Ibrāhīm). So, he is Yūsuf, the son of Ya'qūb, the son of Isḥāq, and the son of Ibrāhīm. Thus, Yūsuf (عَلَيْهِ السَّلَامُ) was a prophet from the descendants of the Prophets. He was the noblest of creation.

They said: "This is not what we are asking you about." So, he responded: ***"Is it the descendants of the Arab that You are asking me about?"***

The descendants of the Arabs mean their foundations and their lineages. He said: ***"The best of them in the pre-Islāmic days of ignorance is the best of them in Islām if they have understanding."***

Meaning: The noblest of people regarding lineage, descendants, and foundations are the best in the pre-Islāmic days of ignorance with the condition they understand.

Example: Banū Hāshim, from what is known, is the best of Quraysh. Therefore, they are the best in Islām, with the condition that they understand Allāh's religion and learn from Allāh's religion; if they were not of those who understand, even if they were the best of the Arabs as far as their descendants, they are not of the noblest of creation with Allāh and are not the best of creation.

This proves that the people are given nobility according to lineage; however, with the condition that they understand Allāh's religion. There is no doubt that lineage has an effect. For this reason, Banū Hāshim was the best of people and the noblest of origins. Thus, the

Messenger of Allāh (صَلَّى ٱللَّٰهُ عَلَيْهِ وَسَلَّمَ) was from them, and he is the noblest of creation. Allāh said:

﴿ٱللَّهُ أَعْلَمُ حَيْثُ يَجْعَلُ﴾

> **"And Allāh knows best with whom He gives His Message."**
> [Sūrah al-Anʿām 6:124]

Had it not been the case that this inner part of the children of Adam was the noblest, the Prophet (صَلَّى ٱللَّٰهُ عَلَيْهِ وَسَلَّمَ) would not have been from them, for the Messenger (صَلَّى ٱللَّٰهُ عَلَيْهِ وَسَلَّمَ) was only sent amongst the most aristocratic and highest of lineages. The point we take from this *Ḥadīth* is the statement of the Messenger (صَلَّى ٱللَّٰهُ عَلَيْهِ وَسَلَّمَ):

> ***"Verily, the noblest of creation are those who have the most Taqwā."***

Hence, if you wish to be noble with Allāh and one who has standing with Him, it is upon you to have *Taqwā*. Whenever someone has the most *Taqwā* of Allāh, he is the noblest with him. I Ask Allāh that He makes you and me from the *Muttaqīn*.

The Second Ḥadīth

«عَنْ أَبِى سَـــعِيدٍ الْخُدْرِيّ ، عَنِ النَّبِيِّ صَلَّى اللَّهُ عَلَيْهِ وَسَلَّمَ قَالَ:
إِنَّ الدُّنْيَا حُلْوَةٌ خَضِرَةٌ، وَإِنَّ اللَّهَ مُسْتَخْلِفُكُمْ فِيهَا، فَيَنْظُرُ كَيْفَ
تَعْمَلُونَ، فَاتَّقُوا الدُّنْيَا وَاتَّقُوا النِّسَـــاءَ، فَإِنَّ أَوَّلَ فِتْنَةِ بَنِي إِسْرَائِيلَ
كَانَتْ فِي النِّسَاءِ " وَفِي حَدِيثِ ابْنِ بَشَّارٍ " لِيَنْظُرَ كَيْفَ تَعْمَلُونَ»

On the authority of Abū Saʿīd al-Khudrī (رَضِيَ ٱللَّهُ عَنْهُ). On the authority of the Prophet (صَلَّى ٱللَّهُ عَلَيْهِ وَسَلَّمَ), he said:

> **"Indeed, the dunya (world) is sweet and green, and Allāh has placed you in it as successors to see how you act. So, beware of the dunya and beware of the women, for verily, the first trial of the children of Israel concerned the women.** [Reported by Muslim]

EXPLANATION

The author (رَحِمَهُ ٱللَّهُ) quoted this *Ḥadīth* because of the command of the Prophet (صَلَّى ٱللَّهُ عَلَيْهِ وَسَلَّمَ) to have *Taqwā*. After he mentioned the condition of this world, he said:

> **"Verily, this world is sweet and green."**

Sweet in its taste and green in its sight. If something is green and sweet, the eye searches for it first; afterward, the self seeks it out. If the searching of the eye and the self are combined in something, a person will likely fall into it.

Thus, this world is sweet in its taste and green in its sight, so people become deceived by it, and it becomes insatiable to them. An individual will make it his most significant importance; however, the Prophet (صَلَّى ٱللَّهُ عَلَيْهِ وَسَلَّمَ) has clarified that Allāh has appointed us as successors coming after each other to look to see how we behave. He said:

"Allāh (سُبْحَانَهُ وَتَعَالَىٰ) has made you successors, one after another, in it to see how you act.

Will you establish His obedience and prevent the self from its desires? Will you fulfill what Allāh has obligated upon you and not be deceived by the worldly life? Or is the matter contrary to that? For this reason, he said:

> **"So, beware of the dunya."**

Meaning: Fulfill what He has ordered you with and leave off with what He has forbidden you from, and do not let the sweetness of this world and its splendor deceive you. Just as Allāh (سُبْحَانَهُ وَتَعَالَىٰ) has said:

﴿فَلَا تَغُرَّنَّكُمُ ٱلْحَيَوٰةُ ٱلدُّنْيَا وَلَا يَغُرَّنَّكُم بِٱللَّهِ ٱلْغَرُورُ ٣٣﴾

> **"Do not let the worldly life deceive you, and do not let the chief deceiver deceive you about Allāh."** [Sūrah Luqmān 31:33]

After that, he said:

> **"So, beware of this world and beware of the women."**

Meaning: Take caution from them.

This includes taking caution from the woman with her cunning towards her husband and taking notice of the women and their trials. For this reason, he said:

> **"For verily, the first trial of the children of Israel was concerning the women."**

Thus, they were tried with the women. They became misguided and misguided others, and Allāh's refuge is sought. For that reason, we find our enemies and the enemies of our religion, the enemies of Allāh's legislation (سُبْحَانَهُ وَتَعَالَى) attaching particular emphasis to the woman. These days, they go out for men to see them beautified, free mix with men, and participate with men in workplaces. It is to the point that people become as though they are donkeys. They merely attach importance to their stomachs and their private parts. Allāh's refuge is sought. The women become as though they are dolls. Meaning: They are like images.

The people only give importance to the image of a woman; how to embellish and beautify them, and how can they bring embellishments and beauty supplies to her; things like hair extensions, piercings, and plastic surgery of the hair, shins, arms, faces, and everything else.

To the point that the most significant importance of the woman is to resemble an image made of plastic. She shows no concern for worship or children. Then, our enemies, the enemies of Allāh's religion and His legislation, the enemies of shyness, look to involve the woman in positions of men; up to a point, they oppress the men and leave the youth wandering about aimlessly in the marketplaces. They have no business there, and there occurs from their free time great evil and a multitude of trials; because the youth, free time, and richness are from the most significant corruptions, as it was said in this line of poetry:

> **"Verily the youth, free time, and his diligence is corruption to the person a great abundance of corruption."**

Thus, they place the woman in manly positions and leave the youth to corrupt them and corrupt the women. Do you know what is taking place?

The corruption of free mixing is taking place by them being in positions with men, along with fornication and despicable sins, whether that be fornication of sight, fornication of the tongue, fornication of the hand, or fornication of the private parts. All of that is conceivable if women are with the men in these positions.

How much corruption has occurred in the lands where the men work with women? After that, if the woman is put in a position, she will be segregated from her home and her husband, and the family will become broken up. The home will need a servant if a position is given to her.

At that point, we will employ the women in the world, from every place, and upon any religion, no matter what their mannerisms are; even if their religion is not the religion of Islām, even if their manners are corrupt, we will employ the woman to be a servant in the homes. We will put our women to work in the places of our men, and we will give our men a leave of absence from work and will employ our women. There is, within this, grand corruption that tears apart the family because if a child is raised and only has the servant in front of him, he will forget his mother and father, and the child's attachment to the two of them will be lost.

The homes would become corrupted, and families would become scattered in many directions. By way of that, there will occur so much corruption that none knows except Allāh. There is no doubt that our enemies and the followers of our enemies; because there are followers of our enemies who study from them and become soiled by their evil ideologies. I do not say that they brainwash them; instead, I say that they have polluted their minds with these despicable ideologies that show resistance to the religion of Islām.

They even say this does not oppose the *'Aqīdah*; on the contrary, we say it *destroys* the *'Aqīdah*. They say that someone says Allāh has a partner or that Allāh is not in existence, and what resembles that does not oppose the *'Aqīdah*; instead, these sins eradicate the *'Aqīdah*; because the people will remain as though they are bulls or donkeys. They attach no importance to the *'Aqīdah* nor to worship; they are attached to this world, its adornments, and the women. There has come in the *Sahīh Ḥadīth*:

«مَا تَرَكْتُ بَعْدِي فِتْنَةً أَضَرَّ عَلَى الرِّجَالِ مِنَ النِّسَاءِ»

> **"I have not left a trial, after me, more harmful upon men than women."**

For this reason, it is obligatory on us, and we, with the praise of Allāh, are a safe nation, to oppose these ideologies. We take a stance in opposition to them in every place and every correlation, knowing that there is with us a people -may Allāh not make them plentiful and may He cause them not to reach their objective- who wish, by this matter, for trials and evil to occur to this safe and peaceful and protected land; because they know that it is the last fortress for the Muslims; this land which contains the sanctuaries of the Muslims and the prayer direction of the Muslims, to corrupt it, up until they corrupt this Islāmic nation. Every Islāmic nation looks to this land and what it is doing because if shyness and religion are destroyed in this land, then they're done for, and the religion and shyness are gone. For this reason, I say: "O my brothers, it is obligatory upon us, upon the youth, the middle age mature ones, our elders, our scholars, and our students of knowledge to oppose these ideologies and establish all the people in its opposition so that the spread of this fire and this foulness does not reach us and destroy us. We ask Allāh (سُبۡحَانَهُۥ وَتَعَالَىٰ) to make the plotting of these, those who dispose of the likeness of these matters in their throats, and that they do not reach the obtainment of the objective, and that he subdues them by way of the righteous men, so their tribulations die. Verily, He is *al-Jawād al-Karīm*.

The Third Ḥadīth

On the authority of Ibn Masʿūd (رَضِيَ اللَّهُ عَنْهُ), the Prophet (صَلَّى اللَّهُ عَلَيْهِ وَسَلَّمَ) used to say:

«اللَّهُمَّ إِنِّي أَسْأَلُكَ الْهُدَى وَالتُّقَى، وَالْعَفَافَ وَالْغِنَى»

"O Allāh. I ask you for guidance, Taqwā, abstinence, and richness." [Reported by Muslim]

EXPLANATION

From the *Ḥadīth*s the author (رَحِمَهُ اللَّهُ) brought in the chapter of *Taqwā* is this *Ḥadīth* that the Prophet (صَلَّى اللَّهُ عَلَيْهِ وَسَلَّمَ) would supplicate to Allāh (سُبْحَانَهُ وَتَعَالَى) with this supplication.

«اللَّهُمَّ إِنِّي أَسْأَلُكَ الْهُدَى وَالتُّقَى، وَالْعَفَافَ وَالْغِنَى»

"O Allāh! I ask you for guidance, Taqwā, abstinence, and richness."

Guidance here takes the meaning of knowledge. The Prophet (ﷺ) needed knowledge just like anyone else, because Allāh (سُبْحَانَهُ وَتَعَالَىٰ) said to him:

﴿وَلَا تَعْجَلْ بِٱلْقُرْءَانِ مِن قَبْلِ أَن يُقْضَىٰٓ إِلَيْكَ وَحْيُهُۥ ۖ وَقُل رَّبِّ زِدْنِى عِلْمًا ﴿١١٤﴾﴾

"Be not in haste [O Muḥammad(ﷺ)] with the Qur'ān before its revelation is completed to you, and say: 'My Lord! Increase me in knowledge.'" [Sūrah at-Taha 9:114]

Also, the Statement of Allāh to His Prophet (ﷺ)

﴿وَعَلَّمَكَ مَا لَمْ تَكُن تَعْلَمُ ۚ وَكَانَ فَضْلُ ٱللَّهِ عَلَيْكَ عَظِيمًا ﴿١١٣﴾﴾

"And He taught you that which you knew not. Ever Great is the Grace of Allāh unto you [O Muḥammad (ﷺ)]" [Sūrah an-Nisā' 4:113]

Thus, he (ﷺ) needed knowledge.

He would ask Allāh for guidance. If guidance is mentioned in isolation, it contains the meaning of knowledge and success to the truth. If it is accompanied by what indicates success to the truth, it bears the meaning of knowledge; because the foundation concerning the Arabic language is that when one word is connected to another word, then it implies that there is a difference, therefore, guidance would have a meaning, and the word the follows it of what points to success takes on a different meaning.

As far as his statement:

«وَالتُّقَى»

"And *Tuqā*."

The meaning of *Tuqā* here: is the *Taqwā* of Allāh (سُبْحَانَهُ وَتَعَالَى).

Therefore, the Prophet (صَلَّى ٱللَّهُ عَلَيْهِ وَسَلَّمَ) would ask his Lord for *Taqwā*. Meaning: He would give him success towards the *Taqwā* of Allāh because Allāh (سُبْحَانَهُ وَتَعَالَى) is the One in Whose Hand is the keys of everything

Thus, if the servant were to be entrusted to himself, he would become wasted, and nothing would occur; if Allāh were to give him success and provide him with *Taqwā*, he would become upright upon the *Taqwā* of Allāh (سُبْحَانَهُ وَتَعَالَى).

As far as his statement:

«وَالْعَفَافَ»

"And *'Afāf* (abstinence)."

The intent is that Allāh would bestow upon him abstinence from doing what is not permissible. Connecting abstinence with the word *Taqwā* is a way of connecting what is specific to what is general. So, abstinence is that he would leave off everything Allāh had made impermissible. *All* of Allāh's prohibitions are included in that.

As for his statement:

«وَالْغِنَى»

"And richness."

The intent of it is to be rich of everything besides Allāh. Meaning: Being free of need from the creation, in as much that he has no need of anyone besides his Lord (سُبْحَانَهُ وَتَعَالَى).

If Allāh was to give the people success and bestow them with no need for the creation, the self would become mighty; they would not be lowly because needing the creation is lowliness and degradation, whereas needing Allāh is strength and worship. Thus he (صَلَّى ٱللَّهُ عَلَيْهِ وَسَلَّمَ) would ask Allāh (سُبْحَانَهُ وَتَعَالَى) for richness.

Thus, we must follow the Messenger (صَلَّى ٱللَّهُ عَلَيْهِ وَسَلَّمَ) in this supplication that we ask Allāh for guidance, *Taqwā*, abstinence, and richness.

This *Ḥadīth* proves that the Prophet (صَلَّى ٱللَّهُ عَلَيْهِ وَسَلَّمَ) has no power of benefit or harm; Allāh is the only one who has that.

It also proves the falsehood of being attached to Allāh's allies and the righteous to obtain benefit and to repel harm, as is the case of some ignorant ones, those who call upon the Messenger (صَلَّى ٱللَّهُ عَلَيْهِ وَسَلَّمَ) while they are at his grave. Or they supplicate to those whom they claim to be of Allāh's allies other than Allāh. These are astray in their religion and foolish in their intellects because the ones who are called upon possess no ability for themselves. Allāh (سُبْحَانَهُ وَتَعَالَى) said to his Prophet (صَلَّى ٱللَّهُ عَلَيْهِ وَسَلَّمَ):

﴿قُل لَّآ أَقُولُ لَكُمْ عِندِى خَزَآئِنُ ٱللَّهِ وَلَآ أَعْلَمُ ٱلْغَيْبَ وَلَآ أَقُولُ لَكُمْ إِنِّى مَلَكٌ﴾

> **"Say, [O Muḥammad (صَلَّى ٱللَّهُ عَلَيْهِ وَسَلَّمَ)]: 'I do not tell you that I have the depositories containing the provision of Allāh, or that I know the unseen, nor do I tell you that I am an angel.'"** [Sūrah al-Anʿām 6:50]

He also said:

﴿قُل لَّآ أَمْلِكُ لِنَفْسِى نَفْعًا وَلَا ضَرًّا إِلَّا مَا شَآءَ ٱللَّهُ﴾

> **"Say, I hold not for myself the power of benefit nor harm except what Allāh has willed."** [Sūrah al-Aʿrāf 7:188]

He also said:

﴿قُلْ إِنِّى لَآ أَمْلِكُ لَكُمْ ضَرًّا وَلَا رَشَدًا ﴿٢١﴾ قُلْ إِنِّى لَن يُجِيرَنِى مِنَ
ٱللَّهِ أَحَدٌ وَلَنْ أَجِدَ مِن دُونِهِۦ مُلْتَحَدًا ﴿٢٢﴾﴾

> **"Say: 'Indeed, I do not possess the power of harm or right direction for you.' Say: 'Indeed, there will never protect me from Allāh anyone if I should disobey nor will I find any other than Him a refuge.'"** [Sūrah al-Jinn 72:21-22]

Therefore, the people must know that whenever somebody comes with esteem from Allāh (سُبْحَانَهُ وَتَعَالَىٰ) and has rank and standing with Him, they do not deserve to be supplicated to other than Allāh; instead, they -and I mean, those who have status with Allāh, from the Prophets and the righteous- that they completely free themselves from those who supplicate to them other than Allāh (سُبْحَانَهُۥ وَتَعَالَىٰ).

ʿĪsā (Jesus عَلَيْهِ ٱلسَّلَامُ) said:

﴿وَإِذْ قَالَ ٱللَّهُ يَٰعِيسَى ٱبْنَ مَرْيَمَ ءَأَنتَ قُلْتَ لِلنَّاسِ ٱتَّخِذُونِى وَأُمِّىَ إِلَٰهَيْنِ مِن دُونِ ٱللَّهِ ۖ قَالَ سُبْحَٰنَكَ مَا يَكُونُ لِىٓ أَنْ أَقُولَ مَا لَيْسَ لِى بِحَقٍّ﴾

> **"When Allāh said to him: 'Did you say to the people, take my mother and me as deities besides Allāh?' He will say: 'Exalted are you; it was not for me to say that to which I have no right.'"** [Sūrah al-Māʾidah 5:116]

Therefore, it is not from the right of ʿĪsā or anyone else to say to the people: "Take me as a deity to be worshipped other than Allāh."

He said:

﴿إِن كُنتُ قُلْتُهُۥ فَقَدْ عَلِمْتَهُۥ ۚ تَعْلَمُ مَا فِى نَفْسِى وَلَآ أَعْلَمُ مَا فِى نَفْسِكَ ۚ إِنَّكَ أَنتَ عَلَّٰمُ ٱلْغُيُوبِ ۝١١٦ مَا قُلْتُ لَهُمْ إِلَّا مَآ أَمَرْتَنِى بِهِۦٓ أَنِ ٱعْبُدُوا۟ ٱللَّهَ رَبِّى وَرَبَّكُمْ﴾

> **"If I had said it, you would have known it. You know what is within me, and I do not know what is within yourself. Indeed. It is You Who is the Knower of the unseen. I said not to them, except what You commanded me, to worship Allāh, my Lord and your Lord."** [Sūrah al-Māʾidah 5:116-117]

In brief: That which we hear amongst the ignorant Muslims in various Islāmic regions, those who go to the graves of those whom they claim to be allies, and they supplicate to these allies. Indeed, this action is foolish in the intellect and is misguidance in the religion. These (the dead) will never help anyone; they are corpses. They cannot move, so how can they cause anything other than themselves to move? Allāh is the grantor of success.

The Fourth Ḥadīth

On the authority of Abū Tarif ʿAdī bin Ḥātim at-Ṭāʾī (رَضِيَ اللَّهُ عَنْهُ), he said: "I heard the Messenger of Allāh (صَلَّى اللَّهُ عَلَيْهِ وَسَلَّمَ) say:

«مَنْ حَلَفَ عَلَى يَمِينٍ، ثُمَّ رَأَى أَتْقَى لِلَّهِ مِنْهَا فَلْيَأْتِ التَّقْوَى»

> **"Whoever swears that he would do something (al-Yamīn), after that, he sees that which has more Taqwā of Allāh than it, let him do that which is of more Taqwā."** [Reported by Muslim]

EXPLANATION

al-Yamīn is to take an oath with Allāh (سُبْحَانَهُ وَتَعَالَى) or by one of His Names or Attributes. It is not permissible to swear by other than Allāh; it is not permitted to swear by the Prophet (صَلَّى اللَّهُ عَلَيْهِ وَسَلَّمَ), Jibrīl (عَلَيْهِ السَّلَامُ) or anyone else from the creation, due to the statement of the Prophet (صَلَّى اللَّهُ عَلَيْهِ وَسَلَّمَ).

> **"Whoever takes an oath, let him swear by Allāh or remain silent."**

He also said:

«مَنْ حَلَفَ بِغَيْرِ اللهِ فَقَدْ كَفَرَ أَوْ أَشْرَكَ»

> **"Whoever swears by other than Allāh has disbelieved or has associated partners with Allāh in worship."**

Therefore, whoever swears by other than Allāh, is a sinner, and that oath is not upon him (to fulfill) because it is an oath that is not contracted, due to the statement of the Prophet (ﷺ):

«مَنْ عَمِلَ عَمَلًا لَيْسَ عَلَيْهِ أَمْرُنَا فَهُوَ رَدٌّ»

> **"Whoever does an action not in accordance with our affair, it is rejected."**

It is not proper for people to swear much. This is the meaning of the statement of Allāh (سُبْحَانَهُ وَتَعَالَىٰ):

﴿وَٱحۡفَظُوٓاْ أَيۡمَٰنَكُمۡ﴾

> **"And guard your oaths."** [Sūrah al-Mā'idah 5:89].

This is according to the opinion of some of the scholars of *Tafsīr* (Explanation of the Qur'ān). This is the meaning of the statement of Allāh (سُبْحَانَهُ وَتَعَالَىٰ):

﴿وَٱحۡفَظُوٓاْ أَيۡمَٰنَكُمۡ﴾

"And guard your oaths." [Sūrah al-Mā'idah 5:89]

According to the opinion of some scholars of *Tafsīr*, they said: **"And guard your oaths."** Means: Do not swear much by Allāh, and if you swear, it is for you to restrict your swearing to the will of Allāh; thus, you should say: "By Allāh! If Allāh wills." This is to take two tremendous benefits.

The first benefit is that what you swore by will be easy for you.

The second benefit: Had you broken the oath, there is no atonement upon you. For whoever swears by Allāh and says: *Inn Shā' Allāh* (if Allāh wills), he has not broken his oath, even if he contradicts that which he swore about. As for swearing, which needs atonement, is swearing for something in the future. As for swearing for something that has preceded, there is no atonement for that; however, if the one who took the oath lied, he is perpetrating sin, and if he was truthful, there is nothing against him.

The likeness of this is if someone were to say: "I swear by Allāh, I did not do such and such." In this circumstance, there is no atonement upon him, whether he spoke truthfully or lied; however, if he was honest that he didn't do something, he is free from sin. Whereas, if he lied and did something, he is committing a sin. As for the oath that requires atonement, it is swearing for something in the future; thus, if you swear for something in the future and say: "By Allāh! I am not doing such and such." Here we say: "If you did it, it is upon you to atone for that, and had you not done it, there is no atonement upon you." "By Allāh! I will not do such a such." This is an oath that is contracted, so if you did do it, it is obligatory upon you to atone; if you didn't do it, there is no atonement upon you.

Is it better that I do that which I swore I would abandon, or is it better for me not to do it? The Prophet (صَلَّى ٱللَّٰهُ عَلَيْهِ وَسَلَّمَ) has clarified in this *Ḥadīth* that if you swore by Allāh and you see other than it to be of more *Taqwā* than it, atone for what you have sworn for and fulfill what is of more *Taqwā*.

So, if one were to say: "I swear by Allāh that I will not speak to such and such a person," meanwhile that individual is a Muslim, it is of the most *Taqwā* for you to speak to him because abandoning the Muslim is not permissible. Speak to him and atone for your oath because this is of the most *Taqwā* of Allāh.

Another example: If you were to say: "I swear by Allāh that I will not visit my family member." We say here that visiting the family is keeping ties, which is obligatory. So, keep the relations with your family and atone for your oath because the Prophet (صَلَّى ٱللَّٰهُ عَلَيْهِ وَسَلَّمَ) said:

> **"He sees other than it to be better, then let him atone for his oath and fulfill that which is better."**

According to this, make your judgment.

In conclusion: We say that swearing by Allāh for something in the past is not sought to make an atonement for because there is no atonement for it; however, either the one who was swearing is safe, or he is sinning. If he lied, he sinned, and if he is truthful, he is safe. In contrast, swearing by Allāh for something in the future is what requires atonement. Thus, if one were to take an oath upon something in the future and contradicted that of which he took an oath, it is obligatory upon him to atone. The exception is if he was to connect his oath to the will of Allāh. So, if he were to say: *Inn Shā' Allāh* (if Allāh wills), this has no atonement, even if he contradicts the oath and Allāh is the giver of success.

The Fifth Ḥadīth

«اتَّقوا الله وَصَلُّوا خَمْسَكمْ وَصُومُوا شَهْرَكُمْ وأَدُّوا زَكاةَ أَمْوَالِكُمْ طَيِّبَةً بِها أَنْفُسُكُمْ وأَطِيعُوا ذَا أَمْرِكُمْ تَدْخُلوا جَنَّةَ رَبِّكُمْ»

On the authority of Abū Umāmah as-Suday al-Ajlān al-Bāhilī (رَضِيَٱللَّهُعَنْهُ), he said: "I heard the Messenger of Allāh (صَلَّىٱللَّهُعَلَيْهِوَسَلَّمَ) address the people in the Farewell Pilgrimage. He said:

> **'Have the Taqwā of Allāh, pray your five prayers, fast your month, pay the Zakāh (obligatory charity) of your wealth, and obey your rulers, you will enter the Jannah of your Lord.'"** [Reported by at-Tirmidhī at the end of the book of Salāh, he said: "This Ḥadīth is Hasan Sahīh."]

EXPLANATION

The sermons of Allāh's Messenger (صَلَّىٱللَّهُعَلَيْهِوَسَلَّمَ) were divided into two types:

1. *Rātibah*: Those that were consistent.
2. *'Āridah*: Those that occurred for a reason.

As for the *Rātibah*, they were the sermons for *Jumu'ah* and the *'Īd*s. He (صَلَّى ٱللَّهُ عَلَيْهِ وَسَلَّمَ) would address the people every *Jumu'ah* and every *'Īd*. The scholars have differed about the sermon of the eclipse prayer. Was it considered *Rātibah* or *'Āridah*? The reason for their difference is that the Eclipse did not occur in the time of the Prophet (صَلَّى ٱللَّهُ عَلَيْهِ وَسَلَّمَ) except once. When he prayed, he stood up and addressed the people. Thus, some scholars hold the opinion that it was considered from the sermons that were *Rātibah*. They said that the foundation the Prophet (صَلَّى ٱللَّهُ عَلَيْهِ وَسَلَّمَ) legislated was established and fixed, and the Eclipse did not happen except for one time where the Prophet (صَلَّى ٱللَّهُ عَلَيْهِ وَسَلَّمَ) would have left off of giving the sermon so that we could say it is from the addresses of *'Āridah*.

Other scholars have said that it is from the sermons of *'Āridah*, which is that if he called to it, the speech would be given; otherwise, it wouldn't. However, the closest position to what is correct is that it is from the sermons that are *Rātibah* that are recommended. Thus, if the people were to pray the Eclipse prayer, the Imām would stand and address the people, remind them, and say that which instills fear, as the Prophet (صَلَّى ٱللَّهُ عَلَيْهِ وَسَلَّمَ) would do.

As for the sermons of *'Āridah*, they are what he would address the people with whenever the need would arise.

For example, his sermon at the time when the people of Burayra imposed a condition, and it was the slave girl that 'Ā'ishah (رَضِيَ ٱللَّهُ عَنْهَا) bought. Their people set the condition that there would be loyalty to them. However, 'Ā'ishah (رَضِيَ ٱللَّهُ عَنْهَا) did not accept that. She informed the Prophet (صَلَّى ٱللَّهُ عَلَيْهِ وَسَلَّمَ), at which point he said:

> **"Take her, free her, and impose the condition for them of loyalty."**

After that, he stood, addressed the people, and informed them that loyalty is for the one who frees another.

Likewise, his sermon when Osama bin Zayd (رَضِيَ ٱللَّهُ عَنْهُ) interceded on behalf of the woman of Makhzūmiyyah who would borrow things and she would refuse to return them. Thereupon, the Prophet (صَلَّى ٱللَّهُ عَلَيْهِ وَسَلَّمَ) commanded that her hand be cut. The Quraysh showed concern over her affair. They requested someone to intercede on her behalf to the Messenger of Allāh (صَلَّى ٱللَّهُ عَلَيْهِ وَسَلَّمَ). They asked for Osama bin Zayd (رَضِيَ ٱللَّهُ عَنْهُ) to intervene, and he thus, did so; however, the Prophet (صَلَّى ٱللَّهُ عَلَيْهِ وَسَلَّمَ) said to him:

«أَتَشْفَعُ فِى حَدٍّ مِنْ حُدُودِ اللهِ تَعَالَى؟»

> **"Do you intercede about a prescribed punishment from Allāh's prescribed punishments?"**

After that, he addressed the people and informed them that some were destroyed before us; if one of their noble ones were to steal, they would leave him be, and if an inferior one stole, they would establish the prescribed punishment upon him.

In the Farewell Pilgrimage, the Prophet (صَلَّى ٱللَّهُ عَلَيْهِ وَسَلَّمَ) addressed the people on the Day of *'Arafah* and the day of slaughtering, meaning the day of 'Īd. He admonished the people and reminded them. This *Khutbah* (sermon) is that which occurs continuously, and it is recommended for the leader of the pilgrims to address the people just as the Prophet (صَلَّى ٱللَّهُ عَلَيْهِ وَسَلَّمَ) addressed them.

From that which he addressed them in his sermon, in the farewell pilgrimage is that he said:

> **"O people! Have the Taqwā of your Lord."**

This is just like the statement of Allāh (سُبْحَانَهُۥ وَتَعَالَىٰ) to all humankind:

﴿يَٰٓأَيُّهَا ٱلنَّاسُ ٱتَّقُوا۟ رَبَّكُمُ﴾

> **"Have the *Taqwā* of your Lord."** [Sūrah an-Nisā' 4:1]

Thus, the Messenger of Allāh (صَلَّى ٱللَّهُ عَلَيْهِ وَسَلَّمَ) commanded all the people to have the *Taqwā* of their Lord, the One who created them, supported them with His favors, and prepared them to accept his message. So, he ordered them to have the *Taqwā* of Allāh.

His statement: ***"And pray your five."***

Meaning: Pray the five prayers Allāh has prescribed upon His Messenger (صَلَّى ٱللَّهُ عَلَيْهِ وَسَلَّمَ).

His statement: ***"And fast your month."*** Meaning: The Month of *Ramadān*.

His statement: ***"Give the Zakāh (obligatory charity) of your wealth."*** Meaning: Give it to those who deserve it, and do not be stingy about it.

His statement: ***"And obey your rulers."***

Meaning: Those whom Allāh has placed as leaders over you. This includes the leaders of districts and lands, and it also consists of the general leader, the leader of the whole country. Therefore, it is obligatory upon the citizens to obey them in what does not involve disobedience to Allāh. As for what is in the disobedience of Allāh, it is not permissible to obey them, even if they command with that, because obedience to the creation does not precede obedience to the Creator (سُبْحَانَهُ وَتَعَالَىٰ)

For this reason, Allāh said:

﴿يَـٰٓأَيُّهَا ٱلَّذِينَ ءَامَنُوٓا۟ أَطِيعُوا۟ ٱللَّهَ وَأَطِيعُوا۟ ٱلرَّسُولَ وَأُو۟لِى ٱلْأَمْرِ مِنكُمْ﴾

> **"O you who believe obey Allāh and obey the Messenger and those in authority amongst you."** [Sūrah an-Nisā' 4:59]

He connected obedience to the rulers with obedience to Allāh and His Messenger (صَلَّى ٱللَّهُ عَلَيْهِ وَسَلَّمَ). This proves that it follows afterward, and it is not independent. For this reason, you see that Allāh says:

﴿أَطِيعُوا۟ ٱللَّهَ وَأَطِيعُوا۟ ٱلرَّسُولَ﴾

> **"Obey Allāh and obey the Messenger."** [Sūrah an-Nisā' 4:59]

He used a verb to clarify, by way of that, that obedience to the Prophet (صَلَّى ٱللَّهُ عَلَيْهِ وَسَلَّمَ) is independent. Meaning: The obligation of obeying Him is independent, just as is the obligation of obeying Allāh. Along with this, obedience to Him is from obligatory obedience to Allāh, as the Prophet (صَلَّى ٱللَّهُ عَلَيْهِ وَسَلَّمَ) only commanded with that which pleases Allāh. As for other than Him, from the rulers, it may be that they order with other than that which pleases Allāh.

For this reason, he made their obedience follow the obedience to Allāh and His Messenger (صَلَّى ٱللَّهُ عَلَيْهِ وَسَلَّمَ). It is not permissible for anyone to disobey the rulers other than disobeying Allāh. He (the disobedient one) thus says: "This is not the religion." Some of the ignorant ones, if the leaders bring a structure that does not oppose the legislation, may say: "It is not binding for me to establish this structure because it is not religion; it is not found in the Book of Allāh (سُبْحَانَهُ وَتَعَالَىٰ) or the Sunnah of His Messenger (صَلَّى ٱللَّهُ عَلَيْهِ وَسَلَّمَ).

This is from his ignorance. Instead, we say that following this structure is found in the Book of Allāh and the Sunnah of the Messenger (صَلَّى ٱللَّهُ عَلَيْهِ وَسَلَّمَ). Allāh says:

﴿يَـٰٓأَيُّهَا ٱلَّذِينَ ءَامَنُوٓا۟ أَطِيعُوا۟ ٱللَّهَ وَأَطِيعُوا۟ ٱلرَّسُولَ وَأُو۟لِى ٱلْأَمْرِ مِنكُمْ﴾

> **"O you who believe, obey Allāh and obey the Messenger, and those in authority from you."** [Sūrah an-Nisā' 4:59]

There has occurred from the Prophet (صَلَّى ٱللَّهُ عَلَيْهِ وَسَلَّمَ) in numerous *Ḥadīth*s that he ordered with obedience to the rulers. This *Ḥadīth* is from them. Therefore, obedience to the rulers in the structure that they bring of what does not oppose the Command of Allāh (سُبْحَانَهُ وَتَعَالَىٰ) and His Messenger (صَلَّى ٱللَّهُ عَلَيْهِ وَسَلَّمَ) is of what Allāh and His Messenger (صَلَّى ٱللَّهُ عَلَيْهِ وَسَلَّمَ) have commanded with. Were we not to obey those in authority in other than that which Allāh (سُبْحَانَهُ وَتَعَالَىٰ) and His Messenger (صَلَّى ٱللَّهُ عَلَيْهِ وَسَلَّمَ) commanded with, there would have been no benefit for the command to obey those in authority because obedience to Allāh (سُبْحَانَهُ وَتَعَالَىٰ) and His Messenger (صَلَّى ٱللَّهُ عَلَيْهِ وَسَلَّمَ) is obligated, whether the rulers' order with that or not. Hence, these matters the Prophet (صَلَّى ٱللَّٰهُ عَلَيْهِ وَسَلَّمَ) has advised within the Farewell Pilgrimage, the *Taqwā* of Allāh, the five prayers, the *Zakāh* (obligatory charity), fasting, and obedience to the rulers, are necessary matters that are obligatory for the people to attach importance to and to follow the command of the Messenger of Allāh (صَلَّى ٱللَّٰهُ عَلَيْهِ وَسَلَّمَ).

And Allāh knows best.

SECTION FOUR

The Benefits of Taqwā From the Noble Qur'ān

Taqwā of Allāh is the Best Provision the Servant Has for the Benefits of His Religion and Worldly Affairs

All praise is due to Allāh; we praise Him and seek His assistance and His forgiveness. We repent to Him and seek refuge with Him from the evils of ourselves and the wickedness of our actions. Whomsoever Allāh guides, there is none to lead astray, and whomever He leads astray, there is no guide for him. I bear witness that none has the right to be worshipped in truth except Allāh, and I bear witness that Muḥammad is His slave and Messenger (May Allāh praise him in the highest gathering, also, his family, his Companions, and whoever follows them with perfection, and give them much peace).

Taqwā is that the servant takes shelter from what is between him and Allāh's punishment by fulfilling His commands and abstaining from His prohibitions until he is upright in Allāh's servitude in truth. *Taqwā* is the religion, all of it. Many benefits in this life and the Hereafter are derived from what is known. We will mention its benefits with the Might of Allāh (سُبْحَانَهُۥ وَتَعَالَىٰ) that we have extracted from the Noble Qur'ān.

✪ BENEFIT 1

It is a means to be guided by the Qur'ān. Allāh (سُبْحَانَهُۥ وَتَعَالَىٰ) said:

﴿ذَٰلِكَ ٱلْكِتَٰبُ لَا رَيْبَ ۛ فِيهِ ۛ هُدًى لِّلْمُتَّقِينَ ۝٢﴾

> **"This is the Book (the Qur'ān), whereof there is no doubt, a guidance to those who are *al-Muttaqūn* [the pious and righteous persons who fear Allāh much (abstain from all kinds of sins and evil deeds which He has forbidden) and love Allāh much (perform all kinds of good deeds which He has ordained)]."** [Sūrah al-Baqarah 2:2]

✪ BENEFIT 2

It is a means for success. Allāh (سُبْحَانَهُۥ وَتَعَالَىٰ) said:

﴿وَأُو۟لَٰٓئِكَ هُمُ ٱلْمُفْلِحُونَ ۝٥﴾

> **"And they are the successful ones."** [Sūrah al-Baqarah 2:5]

✪ BENEFIT 3

It is a means to take benefit from the admonitions.

Allāh (سُبۡحَانَهُۥوَتَعَالَىٰ) said:

﴿فَجَعَلۡنَٰهَا نَكَٰلٗا لِّمَا بَيۡنَ يَدَيۡهَا وَمَا خَلۡفَهَا وَمَوۡعِظَةٗ لِّلۡمُتَّقِينَ ٦٦﴾

> **"So, We made this punishment an example to their own and to succeeding generations and a lesson to those who are *al-Muttaqūn* (the pious)."** [Sūrah al-Baqarah 2:66]

✪ BENEFIT 4

By way of it, along with *Īmān*, the servant will obtain the reward from Allāh.

Allāh (سُبۡحَانَهُۥوَتَعَالَىٰ) said:

﴿وَلَوۡ أَنَّهُمۡ ءَامَنُواْ وَٱتَّقَوۡاْ لَمَثُوبَةٞ مِّنۡ عِندِ ٱللَّهِ خَيۡرٞۚ لَّوۡ كَانُواْ
يَعۡلَمُونَ ١٠٣﴾

> **"And if they had believed, and guarded themselves against evil and kept their duty to Allāh, far better would have been the reward from their Lord if they but knew!"** [Sūrah al-Baqarah 2:103]

✿ BENEFIT 5

That *al-Birr* (piety, righteousness) in truth is what commences from *Taqwā*.

Allāh (سُبْحَانَهُ وَتَعَالَىٰ) said:

﴿وَلَٰكِنَّ ٱلْبِرَّ مَنِ ٱتَّقَىٰ﴾

> **"But *al-Birr* (is the quality of the one) who fears Allāh."** [Sūrah al-Baqarah 2:189]

✿ BENEFIT 6

Taqwā is a reason for success.

Allāh (سُبْحَانَهُ وَتَعَالَىٰ) said:

﴿وَٱتَّقُوا۟ ٱللَّهَ لَعَلَّكُمْ تُفْلِحُونَ ١٨٩﴾

> **"And fear Allāh that you may be successful."** [Sūrah al-Baqarah 2:189]

✿ BENEFIT 7

Through *Taqwā*, you will obtain the specific company of Allāh.

Allāh (سُبْحَانَهُ وَتَعَالَىٰ) said:

﴿وَٱعۡلَمُوٓاْ أَنَّ ٱللَّهَ مَعَ ٱلۡمُتَّقِينَ ١٩٤﴾

"And know that Allāh is with *al-Muttaqūn* (the pious)."
[Sūrah al-Baqarah 2:194]

✪ BENEFIT 8

It is a means of safety from Allāh's punishment.

Allāh (سُبۡحَانَهُۥ وَتَعَالَىٰ) said:

﴿وَٱتَّقُواْ ٱللَّهَ وَٱعۡلَمُوٓاْ أَنَّ ٱللَّهَ شَدِيدُ ٱلۡعِقَابِ ١٩٦﴾

"And fear Allāh much and know that Allāh is Severe in punishment." [Sūrah al-Baqarah 2:196]

✪ BENEFIT 9

It is the best provision.

Allāh (سُبۡحَانَهُۥ وَتَعَالَىٰ) said:

﴿وَتَزَوَّدُواْ فَإِنَّ خَيۡرَ ٱلزَّادِ ٱلتَّقۡوَىٰ﴾

"And take a provision (with you) for the journey, but the

> **best provision is *at-Taqwā* (piety, righteousness, etc.).”** [Sūrah al-Baqarah 2:197]

✪ BENEFIT 10

Those characterized by *Taqwā* are above the rest of the people on the Day of Standing.

Allāh (سُبْحَانَهُ وَتَعَالَىٰ) said:

﴿وَٱلَّذِينَ ٱتَّقَوْا۟ فَوْقَهُمْ يَوْمَ ٱلْقِيَـٰمَةِ﴾

> **“But those who obey Allāh’s Orders and keep away from what He has forbidden will be above them on the Day of Resurrection.”** [Sūrah al-Baqarah 2:212]

✪ BENEFIT 11

It is from the reasons for increased knowledge.

Allāh (سُبْحَانَهُ وَتَعَالَىٰ) said:

﴿وَٱتَّقُوا۟ ٱللَّهَ ۖ وَيُعَلِّمُكُمُ ٱللَّهُ ۗ وَٱللَّهُ بِكُلِّ شَىْءٍ عَلِيمٌ ﴿٢٨٢﴾﴾

> **"So be afraid of Allāh, and Allāh will teach you."** [Sūrah al-Baqarah 2:282]

✿ BENEFIT 12

The reward of those characterized by *Taqwā* is better than this world and all its desires.

Allāh (سُبْحَانَهُ وَتَعَالَى) said:

﴿قُلْ أَؤُنَبِّئُكُم بِخَيْرٍ مِّن ذَٰلِكُمْ ۚ لِلَّذِينَ اتَّقَوْا عِندَ رَبِّهِمْ﴾

> **"Say: 'Shall I inform you of things far better than those? For *al-Muttaqūn* (the pious).'"** [Sūrah āl-'Imrān 3:15]

✿ BENEFIT 13

Their reward is that of gardens under which are the flowing of rivers.

Allāh (سُبْحَانَهُ وَتَعَالَى) said:

﴿جَنَّاتٌ تَجْرِي مِن تَحْتِهَا الْأَنْهَارُ خَالِدِينَ فِيهَا وَأَزْوَاجٌ
مُّطَهَّرَةٌ وَرِضْوَانٌ مِّنَ اللَّهِ﴾

> **"There are Gardens (Paradise) with their Lord, under-**

neath which rivers flow. Therein (is their) eternal (home) and Azwājun Mutahharatun (purified mates or wives) [i.e. they will have no menses, urine, or stool, etc.], and Allāh will be pleased with them.” [Sūrah āl-ʿImrān 3:15]

✿ BENEFIT 14

By way of it, you will obtain Allāh’s Love.

Allāh (سُبْحَانَهُ وَتَعَالَىٰ) said:

﴿بَلَىٰ مَنْ أَوْفَىٰ بِعَهْدِهِۦ وَٱتَّقَىٰ فَإِنَّ ٱللَّهَ يُحِبُّ ٱلْمُتَّقِينَ ٧٦﴾

“Yes, whoever fulfills his pledge and fears Allāh much; verily, then Allāh loves those who are *al-Muttaqūn* (the pious).” [Sūrah āl-ʿImrān 3:76]

✿ BENEFIT 15

It is a means of defense against the enemy.

Allāh (سُبْحَانَهُ وَتَعَالَىٰ) said:

﴿وَإِن تَصْبِرُوا۟ وَتَتَّقُوا۟ لَا يَضُرُّكُمْ كَيْدُهُمْ شَيْـًٔا﴾

> **"But if you remain patient and become *al-Muttaqūn* (the pious), not the least harm will their cunning do to you."** [Sūrah āl-ʿImrān 3:120]

✪ BENEFIT 16

Through *Taqwā* is the actualization of gratitude.

Allāh (سُبْحَانَهُ وَتَعَالَىٰ) said:

﴿فَاتَّقُوا اللَّهَ لَعَلَّكُمْ تَشْكُرُونَ ١٢٣﴾

> **"So, fear Allāh much [abstain from all kinds of sins and evil deeds which He has forbidden and love Allāh much, perform all kinds of good deeds which He has ordained] that you may be grateful."** [Sūrah āl-ʿImrān 3:123]

✪ BENEFIT 17

It is from the reasons for having aid and the Angels reinforcements.

Allāh (سُبْحَانَهُ وَتَعَالَىٰ) said:

﴿بَلَىٰ إِن تَصْبِرُوا وَتَتَّقُوا وَيَأْتُوكُم مِّن فَوْرِهِمْ هَٰذَا يُمْدِدْكُمْ

﴿رَبُّكُم بِخَمْسَةِ ءَالَٰفٍ مِّنَ ٱلْمَلَٰٓئِكَةِ مُسَوِّمِينَ ١٢٥﴾

"Yes, if you hold on to patience and piety, and the enemy comes rushing at you, your Lord will help you with five thousand angels having marks (of distinction)." [Sūrah āl-ʿImrān 3:125]

✪ BENEFIT 18

It is from the reasons for success.

Allāh (سُبْحَانَهُ وَتَعَالَىٰ) said:

﴿وَٱتَّقُوا۟ ٱللَّهَ لَعَلَّكُمْ تُفْلِحُونَ ٢٠٠﴾

"And fear Allāh, so that you may be successful." [Sūrah āl-ʿImrān 3:200]

✪ BENEFIT 19

Allāh has prepared for those characterized with *Taqwā Jannah* (Paradise), whose width is that of the heavens and the earth.

Allāh (سُبْحَانَهُ وَتَعَالَىٰ) said:

﴿وَجَنَّةٍ عَرْضُهَا ٱلسَّمَٰوَٰتُ وَٱلْأَرْضُ أُعِدَّتْ لِلْمُتَّقِينَ ١٣٣﴾

> **"And for Paradise as wide as are the heavens and the earth, prepared for *al-Muttaqūn* (the pious)."** [Sūrah āl-'Imrān 3:133]

✿ BENEFIT 20

It is from the means of obtaining the great reward.

Allāh (سُبْحَانَهُ وَتَعَالَىٰ) said:

﴿لِلَّذِينَ أَحْسَنُوا۟ مِنْهُمْ وَٱتَّقَوْا۟ أَجْرٌ عَظِيمٌ ١٧٢﴾

> **"For those of them who did good deeds and feared Allāh, there is a great reward."** [Sūrah āl-'Imrān 3:172]

Allāh (سُبْحَانَهُ وَتَعَالَىٰ) said:

﴿وَإِن تُؤْمِنُوا۟ وَتَتَّقُوا۟ فَلَكُمْ أَجْرٌ عَظِيمٌ ١٧٩﴾

> **"And if you believe and fear Allāh, then for you, there is a great reward."** [Sūrah āl-'Imrān 3:179]

✿ BENEFIT 21

It is a means of knowledge and being admonished by the Qur'ān.

Allāh (سُبْحَانَهُ وَتَعَالَىٰ) said:

﴿هَٰذَا بَيَانٌ لِّلنَّاسِ وَهُدًى وَمَوْعِظَةٌ لِّلْمُتَّقِينَ ١٣٨﴾

> **"This (the Qur'ān) is a plain statement for mankind, a guidance and instruction to those who are *al-Muttaqūn* (the pious)."** [Sūrah āl-'Imrān 3:138]

✿ BENEFIT 22

Along with patience, it is from the strongest of affairs. It indicates resolve and determination.

Allāh (سُبْحَانَهُ وَتَعَالَىٰ) said:

﴿وَإِن تَصْبِرُوا۟ وَتَتَّقُوا۟ فَإِنَّ ذَٰلِكَ مِنْ عَزْمِ ٱلْأُمُورِ ١٨٦﴾

> **"But if you persevere patiently and become *al-Muttaqūn* (the pious), then verily, that will be a determining factor in all affairs, and that is from the great matters, [which you must hold on with all your efforts]."** [Sūrah āl-'Imrān 3:186]

✪ BENEFIT 23

Those characterized by *Taqwā* have gardens under which rivers flow.

Allāh (سُبْحَانَهُ وَتَعَالَىٰ) said:

﴿لَٰكِنِ ٱلَّذِينَ ٱتَّقَوْا۟ رَبَّهُمْ لَهُمْ جَنَّٰتٌ تَجْرِى
مِن تَحْتِهَا ٱلْأَنْهَٰرُ خَٰلِدِينَ فِيهَا﴾

> **"But, for those who fear their Lord, are Gardens under which rivers flow (in Paradise); therein are they to dwell (forever)."** [Sūrah āl-ʿImrān 3:198]

✪ BENEFIT 24

It is from the means of success.

Allāh (سُبْحَانَهُ وَتَعَالَىٰ) said:

﴿وَٱتَّقُوا۟ ٱللَّهَ لَعَلَّكُمْ تُفْلِحُونَ ١٨٩﴾

> **"And fear Allāh that you may be successful."** [Sūrah al-Baqarah 2:189]

✪ BENEFIT 25

The Hereafter is better than this world for the *Muttaqīn* (those characterized by *Taqwā*).

Allāh (سُبْحَانَهُ وَتَعَالَىٰ) said:

﴿وَٱلْأَخِرَةُ خَيْرٌ لِّمَنِ ٱتَّقَىٰ﴾

"The Hereafter is (far) better for him who fears Allāh." [Sūrah an-Nisā' 4:77]

✪ BENEFIT 26

It is from the means of forgiveness and mercy.

Allāh (سُبْحَانَهُ وَتَعَالَىٰ) said:

﴿وَإِن تُصْلِحُوا۟ وَتَتَّقُوا۟ فَإِنَّ ٱللَّهَ كَانَ غَفُورًا رَّحِيمًا ١٢٩﴾

"And if you do justice and do all that is right and fear Allāh by keeping away from all that is wrong, then Allāh is Ever Oft-Forgiving, Most Merciful." [Sūrah an-Nisā' 4:129]

✪ BENEFIT 27

It is from the means for the acceptance of actions.

Allāh (سُبۡحَانَهُۥوَتَعَالَىٰ) said:

﴿قَالَ إِنَّمَا يَتَقَبَّلُ ٱللَّهُ مِنَ ٱلۡمُتَّقِينَ ٢٧﴾

> **"The former said: "Verily, Allāh accepts only from those who are *al-Muttaqūn* (the pious)."** [Sūrah al-Mā'idah 5:27]

✪ BENEFIT 28

It is from the means of success.

Allāh (سُبۡحَانَهُۥوَتَعَالَىٰ) said:

﴿ٱتَّقُواْ ٱللَّهَ وَٱبۡتَغُوٓاْ إِلَيۡهِ ٱلۡوَسِيلَةَ وَجَٰهِدُواْ فِي
سَبِيلِهِۦ لَعَلَّكُمۡ تُفۡلِحُونَ ٣٥﴾

> **"Do your duty to Allāh, fear Him, seek the means of approach to Him, and strive hard for His Cause as much as possible. So that you may be successful."** [Sūrah al-Mā'idah 5:35]

✿ BENEFIT 29

Those characterized by it receive benefit from the Divine Books in guidance and admonition.

Allāh (سُبْحَانَهُ وَتَعَالَىٰ) said:

﴿وَءَاتَيْنَٰهُ ٱلْإِنجِيلَ فِيهِ هُدًى وَنُورٌ وَمُصَدِّقًا لِّمَا بَيْنَ يَدَيْهِ
مِنَ ٱلتَّوْرَىٰةِ وَهُدًى وَمَوْعِظَةً لِّلْمُتَّقِينَ ٤٦﴾

> **"And We gave him the Injīl (Gospel), in which was guidance and light and confirmation of the Tawrāh (Torah) that had come before it, a guidance and an admonition for *al-Muttaqūn* (the pious)."** [Sūrah al-Mā'idah 5:46]

✿ BENEFIT 30

It is from the reasons for removing sins and entrance into the Gardens.

Allāh (سُبْحَانَهُ وَتَعَالَىٰ) said:

﴿وَلَوْ أَنَّ أَهْلَ ٱلْكِتَٰبِ ءَامَنُوا۟ وَٱتَّقَوْا۟ لَكَفَّرْنَا عَنْهُمْ
سَيِّـَٔاتِهِمْ وَلَأَدْخَلْنَٰهُمْ جَنَّٰتِ ٱلنَّعِيمِ ٦٥﴾

> **"And if only the people of the Scripture (Jews and Christians) had believed (in Muḥammad صَلَّىٰ ٱللَّهُ عَلَيْهِ وَسَلَّمَ) and warded**

> **off evil (sin, ascribing partners to Allāh) and had become *al-Muttaqūn* (the pious) We would indeed have blotted out their sins and admitted them to Gardens of pleasure (in Paradise).”** [Sūrah al-Mā’idah 5:65]

✪ BENEFIT 31

It is from the reasons for removing sin in what was eaten.

Allāh (سُبۡحَانَهُۥ وَتَعَالَىٰ) said:

﴿لَيۡسَ عَلَى ٱلَّذِينَ ءَامَنُواْ وَعَمِلُواْ ٱلصَّٰلِحَٰتِ جُنَاحٞ فِيمَا طَعِمُوٓاْ إِذَا مَا ٱتَّقَواْ﴾

> **“Those who believe and do righteous good deeds have no sin on them for what they ate (in the past) if they fear Allāh.”** [Sūrah al-Mā’idah 5:93]

✪ BENEFIT 32

It is from the signs of *Īmān*.

Allāh (سُبۡحَانَهُۥ وَتَعَالَىٰ) said:

﴿قَالَ ٱتَّقُواْ ٱللَّهَ إِن كُنتُم مُّؤۡمِنِينَ ١١٢﴾

> **“‘Īsā (Jesus) said: ‘Fear Allāh if you are indeed believers.’”**
> [Sūrah al-Mā’idah 5:112]

✿ BENEFIT 33

The Hereafter is better than this world for the *Muttaqīn*.

Allāh (سُبْحَانَهُ وَتَعَالَىٰ) said:

﴿وَلَلدَّارُ ٱلْآخِرَةُ خَيْرٌ لِّلَّذِينَ يَتَّقُونَ﴾

"But far better is the house in the Hereafter for those who are *al-Muttaqūn* (the pious)." [Sūrah al-Anʿām 6:32]

✿ BENEFIT 34

Those characterized by it have safety from the sin of delving into Allāh's signs.

Allāh (سُبْحَانَهُ وَتَعَالَىٰ) said:

﴿وَإِذَا رَأَيْتَ ٱلَّذِينَ يَخُوضُونَ فِىٓ ءَايَٰتِنَا فَأَعْرِضْ عَنْهُمْ حَتَّىٰ يَخُوضُوا۟ فِى حَدِيثٍ غَيْرِهِۦ ۚ وَإِمَّا يُنسِيَنَّكَ ٱلشَّيْطَٰنُ فَلَا تَقْعُدْ بَعْدَ ٱلذِّكْرَىٰ مَعَ ٱلْقَوْمِ ٱلظَّٰلِمِينَ ﴿٦٨﴾ وَمَا عَلَى ٱلَّذِينَ يَتَّقُونَ مِنْ حِسَابِهِم مِّن شَىْءٍ﴾

"And when you (Muḥammad صَلَّى ٱللَّهُ عَلَيْهِ وَسَلَّمَ) see those who engage in a false conversation about Our Verses (of the Qur'ān) by mocking at them, stay away from them till they turn to another topic. And if *Shayṭān* (Satan) causes

> **you to forget, then after the remembrance, sit not you in the company of those people who are the *Zālimūn* (polytheists and wrongdoers, etc.). Those who fear Allāh, keep their duty to Him and avoid evil are not responsible for them (the disbelievers) in any case."** [Sūrah al-An'ām 6:68-69]

✪ BENEFIT 35

It is from the reasons for mercy.

Allāh (سُبْحَانَهُ وَتَعَالَىٰ) said:

﴿فَٱتَّبِعُوهُ وَٱتَّقُواْ لَعَلَّكُمۡ تُرۡحَمُونَ ١٥٥﴾

> **"So, follow it and fear Allāh (i.e. do not disobey His Orders), that you may receive mercy (i.e. saved from the torment of Hell)."** [Sūrah al-An'ām 6:155]

✪ BENEFIT 36

The clothing of *Taqwā* is the best.

Allāh (سُبْحَانَهُ وَتَعَالَىٰ) said:

﴿وَلِبَاسُ ٱلتَّقۡوَىٰ ذَٰلِكَ خَيۡرٌ﴾

"And the clothing of righteousness, that is better." [Sūrah al-A'rāf 7:26]

✪ BENEFIT 37

It is from the means for the non-existence of fear and sadness.

Allāh (سُبْحَانَهُ وَتَعَالَىٰ) said:

﴿فَمَنِ ٱتَّقَىٰ وَأَصْلَحَ فَلَا خَوْفٌ عَلَيْهِمْ وَلَا هُمْ يَحْزَنُونَ ٣٥﴾

"Then whosoever becomes pious and righteous, on them shall be no fear, nor shall they grieve." [Sūrah al-A'rāf 7:35]

✪ BENEFIT 38

It is a reason for blessings to descend from the sky and arise from the earth.

Allāh (سُبْحَانَهُ وَتَعَالَىٰ) said:

﴿وَلَوْ أَنَّ أَهْلَ ٱلْقُرَىٰٓ ءَامَنُوا۟ وَٱتَّقَوْا۟ لَفَتَحْنَا عَلَيْهِم بَرَكَـٰتٍ
مِّنَ ٱلسَّمَآءِ وَٱلْأَرْضِ﴾

"And if the people of the towns had believed and had the

***Taqwā* (piety), certainly, We should have opened blessings from the heavens and the earth for them.”** [Sūrah al-Aʿrāf 7:96]

✪ BENEFIT 39

The praiseworthy ending result is for the *Muttaqīn*.

Allāh (سُبْحَانَهُ وَتَعَالَىٰ) said:

﴿وَٱلْعَـٰقِبَةُ لِلْمُتَّقِينَ ١٢٨﴾

“And the (blessed) end is for the *Muttaqūn* (pious).”
[Sūrah al-Aʿrāf 7:128]

✪ BENEFIT 40

Taqwā is from the means of mercy.

Allāh (سُبْحَانَهُ وَتَعَالَىٰ) said:

﴿وَرَحْمَتِى وَسِعَتْ كُلَّ شَىْءٍ ۚ فَسَأَكْتُبُهَا لِلَّذِينَ يَتَّقُونَ﴾

“That (Mercy) I shall ordain for those who are the *Muttaqūn* (pious).” [Sūrah al-Aʿrāf 7:156]

✪ BENEFIT 41

The Hereafter is better than this world for the *Muttaqīn*.

Allāh (سُبْحَانَهُۥ وَتَعَالَىٰ) said:

﴿وَٱلدَّارُ ٱلْـَٔاخِرَةُ خَيْرٌ لِّلَّذِينَ يَتَّقُونَ﴾

> **"And the home of the Hereafter is better for those who are *al-Muttaqūn* (the pious)."** [Sūrah al-Aʿrāf 7:169]

✪ BENEFIT 42

Taqwā is a reason for remembrance and clear insight when it comes to the inclinations of Shayṭān.

Allāh (سُبْحَانَهُۥ وَتَعَالَىٰ) said:

﴿إِنَّ ٱلَّذِينَ ٱتَّقَوْا۟ إِذَا مَسَّهُمْ طَٰٓئِفٌ مِّنَ ٱلشَّيْطَٰنِ تَذَكَّرُوا۟ فَإِذَا هُم مُّبْصِرُونَ ٢٠١﴾

> **"Verily, those who are *al-Muttaqūn*, when an evil thought comes to them from *Shayṭān* (Satan), they remember (Allāh), and (indeed) they then see (aright)."** [Sūrah al-Aʿrāf 7: 201]

✿ BENEFIT 43

Taqwā is a reason for clear insight and a criterion to judge between truth and falsehood, and it removes sins and brings about forgiveness. Allāh (E) said:

﴿يَا أَيُّهَا الَّذِينَ آمَنُوا إِن تَتَّقُوا اللَّهَ يَجْعَل لَّكُمْ فُرْقَانًا وَيُكَفِّرْ
عَنكُمْ سَيِّئَاتِكُمْ وَيَغْفِرْ لَكُمْ ۗ وَاللَّهُ ذُو الْفَضْلِ الْعَظِيمِ ٢٩﴾

> **"O you who believe! If you obey and fear Allāh, He will grant you Furqan a criterion [(to judge between right and wrong), or (*Makhraj*, i.e. make a way for you to get out from every difficulty)]. He will expiate for you your sins and forgive you, and Allāh is the Owner of the Great Bounty."** [Sūrah al-Anfāl 8:29]

✿ BENEFIT 44

Those characterized by it are the maintainers and protectors of al-Masjid al-Haram.

Allāh (سُبْحَانَهُ وَتَعَالَىٰ) said:

﴿وَمَا لَهُمْ أَلَّا يُعَذِّبَهُمُ اللَّهُ وَهُمْ يَصُدُّونَ عَنِ الْمَسْجِدِ الْحَرَامِ وَمَا كَانُوا
أَوْلِيَاءَهُ ۚ إِنْ أَوْلِيَاؤُهُ إِلَّا الْمُتَّقُونَ وَلَٰكِنَّ أَكْثَرَهُمْ لَا يَعْلَمُونَ ٣٤﴾

> **"And why should not Allāh punish them while they stop**

(men) from al-Masjid al-Haram, and they are not its guardians? None can be its guardian except *al-Muttaqūn* (the pious), but most of them know not." [Sūrah al-Anfāl 8:34]

✪ BENEFIT 45

Taqwā is a reason for forgiveness and mercy.

Allāh (سُبْحَانَهُ وَتَعَالَىٰ) said:

﴿طَيِّبًاۚ وَٱتَّقُواْ ٱللَّهَۚ إِنَّ ٱللَّهَ غَفُورٞ رَّحِيمٞ ٦٩﴾

"Be afraid of Allāh. Certainly, Allāh is Oft-Forgiving, Most Merciful." [Sūrah al-Anfāl 8:69]

✪ BENEFIT 46

By way of *Taqwā*, you will obtain Allāh's love.

Allāh (سُبْحَانَهُ وَتَعَالَىٰ) said:

﴿إِنَّ ٱللَّهَ يُحِبُّ ٱلۡمُتَّقِينَ ٤﴾

"Surely Allāh loves *al-Muttaqūn* (the pious)" [Sūrah at-Tawbah 9:4]

✪ BENEFIT 47

By way of it, you will obtain Allāh's love.

Allāh (سُبْحَانَهُ وَتَعَالَىٰ) said:

﴿فَٱسْتَقِيمُوا۟ لَهُمْ ۚ إِنَّ ٱللَّهَ يُحِبُّ ٱلْمُتَّقِينَ ۝٧﴾

> **"How can there be a covenant with Allāh and with His Messenger for the *Mushrikūn* (polytheists, idolaters, pagans, disbelievers in the Oneness of Allāh) except those with whom you made a covenant near al-Masjid al-Haram (at Makkah)? So long as they are true to you, stand true to them. Verily, Allāh loves *al-Muttaqūn* (the pious)."** [Surah Sūrah at-Tawbah 9:7]

✪ BENEFIT 48

By way of *Taqwā*, you will obtain the specific company of Allāh.

Allāh (سُبْحَانَهُ وَتَعَالَىٰ) said:

﴿وَٱعْلَمُوٓا۟ أَنَّ ٱللَّهَ مَعَ ٱلْمُتَّقِينَ ۝٣٦﴾

> **"But know that Allāh is with those who are *al-Muttaqūn* (the pious)."** [Sūrah at-Tawbah 9:36]

✪ BENEFIT 49

That which is established upon *Taqwā* has more right than other than it regarding the *Salāh* (Prayer).

Allāh (سُبْحَانَهُ وَتَعَالَىٰ) said:

﴿لَّمَسْجِدٌ أُسِّسَ عَلَى ٱلتَّقْوَىٰ مِنْ أَوَّلِ يَوْمٍ أَحَقُّ أَن تَقُومَ فِيهِ﴾

> **"Verily, the mosque whose foundation was laid from the first day on piety is more worthy that you stand therein (to pray)."** [Sūrah at-Tawbah 9:108]

✪ BENEFIT 50

Good is found in the one who establishes his structure upon *Taqwā*.

Allāh (سُبْحَانَهُ وَتَعَالَىٰ) said:

﴿أَفَمَنْ أَسَّسَ بُنْيَٰنَهُۥ عَلَىٰ تَقْوَىٰ مِنَ ٱللَّهِ وَرِضْوَٰنٍ خَيْرٌ أَم مَّنْ
أَسَّسَ بُنْيَٰنَهُۥ عَلَىٰ شَفَا جُرُفٍ هَارٍ فَٱنْهَارَ بِهِۦ فِى نَارِ جَهَنَّمَ﴾

> **"Is it then he, who laid the foundation of his building on piety to Allāh and His Good Pleasure, better, or he who laid the foundation of his building on an undetermined**

> **brink of a precipice ready to crumble down, so that it crumbled to pieces with him into the Fire of Hell.”** [Sūrah at-Tawbah 9:109]

✪ BENEFIT 51

Taqwā prevents you from seeking permission in Jihad, and by way of it, you will obtain the specific company of Allāh.

Allāh (سُبْحَانَهُ وَتَعَالَىٰ) said:

﴿وَلْيَجِدُوا۟ فِيكُمْ غِلْظَةً ۚ وَٱعْلَمُوٓا۟ أَنَّ ٱللَّهَ مَعَ ٱلْمُتَّقِينَ ۝١٢٣﴾

> **“And let them find harshness in you and know that Allāh is with those who are the *al-Muttaqūn* (the pious).”** [Sūrah at-Tawbah 9:123]

✪ BENEFIT 52

Taqwā is of the means for taking benefit from Allāh’s signs.

Allāh (سُبْحَانَهُ وَتَعَالَىٰ) said:

﴿إِنَّ فِى ٱخْتِلَـٰفِ ٱلَّيْلِ وَٱلنَّهَارِ وَمَا خَلَقَ ٱللَّهُ فِى ٱلسَّمَـٰوَٰتِ
وَٱلْأَرْضِ لَـَٔايَـٰتٍ لِّقَوْمٍ يَتَّقُونَ ۝٦﴾

"Verily, in the alternation of the night and the day and in all that Allāh has created in the heavens and the earth are Ayat (proofs, evidence, verses, lessons, signs, revelations, etc.) for those people who keep their duty to Allāh and fear Him much." [Sūrah Yūnus 10:6]

✪ BENEFIT 53

It is from the means of obtaining Allāh's friendship, and it expels sadness and fear.

Allāh (سُبْحَانَهُ وَتَعَالَىٰ) said:

﴿أَلَآ إِنَّ أَوْلِيَآءَ ٱللَّهِ لَا خَوْفٌ عَلَيْهِمْ وَلَا هُمْ يَحْزَنُونَ ۝٦٢ ٱلَّذِينَ ءَامَنُوا۟ وَكَانُوا۟ يَتَّقُونَ ۝٦٣﴾

"No doubt! Verily, the *Awliyā'* of Allāh [i.e. those who believe in the Oneness of Allāh and fear Allāh much (abstain from all kinds of sins and evil deeds which he has forbidden), and love Allāh much (perform all kinds of good deeds which He has ordained)], no fear shall come upon them, nor shall they grieve." [Sūrah Yūnus 10:62-63]

✪ BENEFIT 54

Those characterized by it have Glad Tidings in this world and the Hereafter.

Allāh (سُبۡحَانَهُۥ وَتَعَالَىٰ) said:

﴿ٱلَّذِينَ ءَامَنُواْ وَكَانُواْ يَتَّقُونَ ٦٣ لَهُمُ ٱلۡبُشۡرَىٰ فِي ٱلۡحَيَوٰةِ ٱلدُّنۡيَا وَفِي ٱلۡأٓخِرَةِۚ لَا تَبۡدِيلَ لِكَلِمَٰتِ ٱللَّهِۚ ذَٰلِكَ هُوَ ٱلۡفَوۡزُ ٱلۡعَظِيمُ ٦٤﴾

> **"Those who believed (in the Oneness of Allāh - Islāmic Monotheism) and used to fear Allāh much (by abstaining from evil deeds and sins and by doing righteous deeds)."** [Sūrah Yūnus 10:63-64]

✿ BENEFIT 55

The praiseworthy outcome is for the *Muttaqīn*.

Allāh (سُبۡحَانَهُۥ وَتَعَالَىٰ) said:

﴿فَٱصۡبِرۡۖ إِنَّ ٱلۡعَٰقِبَةَ لِلۡمُتَّقِينَ ٤٩﴾

> **"So be patient. Surely, the (good) end is for the *Muttaqūn* (pious)"** [Sūrah Hūd 11:49]

✪ BENEFIT 56

Taqwā is a reason for the prevention of enmity.

Allāh (سُبْحَانَهُ وَتَعَالَىٰ) said:

﴿فَاتَّقُوا اللَّهَ وَلَا تُخْزُونِ فِي ضَيْفِي﴾

"So, fear Allāh and degrade me not as regards my guests!"
[Sūrah Hūd 11:78]

✪ BENEFIT 57

The reward of those characterized by it is better than everything in this world.

Allāh (سُبْحَانَهُ وَتَعَالَىٰ) said:

﴿وَلَأَجْرُ الْآخِرَةِ خَيْرٌ لِّلَّذِينَ آمَنُوا وَكَانُوا يَتَّقُونَ ۝٥٧﴾

"And verily, the reward of the Hereafter is better for those who believe and used to fear Allāh and keep their duty to Him (by abstaining from all kinds of sins and evil deeds and by performing all kinds of righteous good deeds)." [Sūrah Yūsuf 12:57]

✪ BENEFIT 58

Taqwā is from perfection, which Allāh will not render to waste the reward of the one endowed with it; from it, He will give preference to him over anyone else.

Allāh (سُبۡحَانَهُۥ وَتَعَالَىٰ) said:

﴿إِنَّهُۥ مَن يَتَّقِ وَيَصۡبِرۡ فَإِنَّ ٱللَّهَ لَا يُضِيعُ أَجۡرَ ٱلۡمُحۡسِنِينَ ٩٠﴾

> **"Verily, he who fears Allāh with obedience to Him (by abstaining from sins and evil deeds, and by performing righteous good deeds), and is patient, then surely, Allāh makes not the reward of the *Muhsinūn* (good-doers) to be lost."**
> [Sūrah Yūsuf 12:90]

✪ BENEFIT 59

The Hereafter is better than this world for the *Muttaqīn*.

Allāh (سُبۡحَانَهُۥ وَتَعَالَىٰ) said:

﴿وَلَدَارُ ٱلۡأٓخِرَةِ خَيۡرٞ لِّلَّذِينَ ٱتَّقَوۡاْ﴾

> **"And verily, the home of the Hereafter is the best for those who fear Allāh and obey Him (by abstaining from sins and evil deeds, and by performing righteous good deeds)."**
> [Sūrah Yūsuf 12:109]

✪ BENEFIT 60

The outcome for the *Muttaqīn* is *Jannah*.

Allāh (سُبْحَانَهُ وَتَعَالَىٰ) said:

﴿مَّثَلُ ٱلْجَنَّةِ ٱلَّتِى وُعِدَ ٱلْمُتَّقُونَ ۖ تَجْرِى مِن تَحْتِهَا ٱلْأَنْهَـٰرُ ۖ أُكُلُهَا دَآئِمٌ وَظِلُّهَا ۚ تِلْكَ عُقْبَى ٱلَّذِينَ ٱتَّقَوا۟ ﴾

"The description of the Paradise which the *Muttaqūn* (the pious): have been promised! -Underneath its rivers flow, its provision is eternal, and so is its shade. This is the end (final destination) of the *Muttaqūn*." [Sūrah ar-Raʿd 13:35]

✪ BENEFIT 61

The reward of those characterized with *Taqwā* is Gardens, by which various forms of delight are within them.

Allāh (سُبْحَانَهُ وَتَعَالَىٰ) said:

﴿إِنَّ ٱلْمُتَّقِينَ فِى جَنَّـٰتٍ وَعُيُونٍ ﴿٤٥﴾ ٱدْخُلُوهَا بِسَلَـٰمٍ ءَامِنِينَ ﴿٤٦﴾ وَنَزَعْنَا مَا فِى صُدُورِهِم مِّنْ غِلٍّ إِخْوَٰنًا عَلَىٰ سُرُرٍ مُّتَقَـٰبِلِينَ ﴿٤٧﴾ لَا يَمَسُّهُمْ فِيهَا نَصَبٌ وَمَا هُم مِّنْهَا بِمُخْرَجِينَ ﴿٤٨﴾ ﴾

"Truly! The *Muttaqūn* (the pious and righteous persons) will be amidst Gardens and water springs (Paradise)." [Sūrah al-Ḥijr 15:45-48]

✪ BENEFIT 62

By way of *Taqwā*, you will know the reality of what Allāh has sent down.

Allāh (سُبْحَانَهُۥوَتَعَالَىٰ) said:

﴿وَقِيلَ لِلَّذِينَ ٱتَّقَوْاْ مَاذَآ أَنزَلَ رَبُّكُمْۚ قَالُواْ خَيْرًا﴾

"And (when) it is said to those who are the *Muttaqūn* (the pious) 'What is it that your Lord has sent down?' They say: 'That which is good.'" [Sūrah an-Naḥl 16:30]

✪ BENEFIT 63

Allāh has praised the abode of the *Muttaqīn* of what indicates to the completeness of its bliss.

Allāh (سُبْحَانَهُۥوَتَعَالَىٰ) said:

﴿وَلَدَارُ ٱلْأَخِرَةِ خَيْرٌۚ وَلَنِعْمَ دَارُ ٱلْمُتَّقِينَ ۝٣٠﴾

> **"The home of the Hereafter will be better. And excellent indeed will be the home (i.e. Paradise) of the *Muttaqūn* (the pious)."** [Sūrah an-Naḥl 16:30]

✪ BENEFIT 64

Those characterized with *Taqwā* will die in the best of circumstances and they will be received with the *Salām* (The greetings of *Salām*) and nobility from the angels.

Allāh (سُبْحَانَهُ وَتَعَالَىٰ) said:

﴿يَشَآءُونَۚ كَذَٰلِكَ يَجۡزِي ٱللَّهُ ٱلۡمُتَّقِينَ ٣١ ٱلَّذِينَ تَتَوَفَّىٰهُمُ ٱلۡمَلَٰٓئِكَةُ
طَيِّبِينَ يَقُولُونَ سَلَٰمٌ عَلَيۡكُمُ ٱدۡخُلُواْ ٱلۡجَنَّةَ بِمَا كُنتُمۡ تَعۡمَلُونَ ٣٢﴾

> **"Thus, Allāh rewards the *Muttaqūn* (the pious). Those whose lives the angels take while they are in a pious state (i.e. pure from all evil, and worshipping none but Allāh Alone) saying (to them): *Salāmun 'Alaikum* (peace be on you) enter you Paradise, because of (the good) which you used to do (in the world)."** [Sūrah an-Naḥl 16:31-32]

✪ BENEFIT 65

Taqwā is from the means of having Allāh's specific company.

Allāh (سُبْحَانَهُ وَتَعَالَىٰ) said:

﴿إِنَّ ٱللَّهَ مَعَ ٱلَّذِينَ ٱتَّقَوا۟ وَّٱلَّذِينَ هُم مُّحْسِنُونَ ١٢٨﴾

> **"Truly, Allāh is with those who fear Him (keep their duty unto Him), and those who are *Muhsinūn* (good-doers)."** [Sūrah an-Naḥl 16:128]

✪ BENEFIT 66

Taqwā is from the descriptions of the Messengers.

Allāh (سُبْحَانَهُ وَتَعَالَىٰ) said:

﴿وَحَنَانًا مِّن لَّدُنَّا وَزَكَوٰةً ۖ وَكَانَ تَقِيًّا ١٣﴾

> **"And (made him) sympathetic to men as a mercy (or a grant) from Us, and pure from sins [i.e. Yaḥyā (John)] and he was righteous."** [Sūrah Maryam 19:13]

✪ BENEFIT 67

By way of *Taqwā* is the inheritance of gardens.

Allāh (سُبْحَانَهُ وَتَعَالَىٰ) said:

﴿تِلْكَ ٱلْجَنَّةُ ٱلَّتِى نُورِثُ مِنْ عِبَادِنَا مَن كَانَ تَقِيًّا ﴿٦٣﴾﴾

> **"Such is the Paradise which We shall give as an inheritance to those of Our slaves who have been *al-Muttaqūn* (pious and righteous persons)."** [Sūrah Maryam 19:63]

✪ BENEFIT 68

It is a reason for safety from the Hellfire.

Allāh (سُبْحَانَهُ وَتَعَالَىٰ) said:

﴿ثُمَّ نُنَجِّى ٱلَّذِينَ ٱتَّقَوا۟ وَّنَذَرُ ٱلظَّـٰلِمِينَ فِيهَا جِثِيًّا ﴿٧٢﴾﴾

> **"Then We shall save those who use to fear Allāh and were dutiful to Him. And We shall leave the *Zālimūn* (polytheists and wrongdoers, etc.) therein (humbled) to their knees (in Hell)."** [Sūrah Maryam 19:72]

✪ BENEFIT 69

Those characterized with it will be gathered being delegated before Allāh with nobility.

Allāh (سُبْحَانَهُ وَتَعَالَىٰ) said:

﴿يَوۡمَ نَحۡشُرُ ٱلۡمُتَّقِينَ إِلَى ٱلرَّحۡمَٰنِ وَفۡدٗا ﴿٨٥﴾﴾

"The Day We shall gather the *Muttaqūn* (the pious) unto the Most Beneficent (Allāh), like a delegate (presented before a king for honor)." [Sūrah Maryam 19:85]

✪ BENEFIT 70

The Qur'ān is a glad tiding for the *Muttaqīn*.

Allāh (سُبۡحَانَهُۥ وَتَعَالَىٰ) said:

﴿لِتُبَشِّرَ بِهِ ٱلۡمُتَّقِينَ﴾

"That you may give glad tidings to the *Muttaqūn* (pious and righteous persons)" [Sūrah Maryam 19:97]

✪ BENEFIT 71

The praiseworthy ending result is for *Taqwā*.

Allāh (سُبۡحَانَهُۥ وَتَعَالَىٰ) said:

﴿وَٱلۡعَٰقِبَةُ لِلتَّقۡوَىٰ ﴿١٣٢﴾﴾

> **"And the good end (i.e. Paradise) is for the *Muttaqūn* (the pious)."** [Sūrah Ṭā-Hā 20:132]

✪ BENEFIT 72

Those characterized by it are those who take benefit from the books.

Allāh (سُبْحَانَهُ وَتَعَالَىٰ) said:

﴿وَلَقَدْ ءَاتَيْنَا مُوسَىٰ وَهَٰرُونَ ٱلْفُرْقَانَ وَضِيَآءً وَذِكْرًا لِّلْمُتَّقِينَ ﴿٤٨﴾﴾

> **"And indeed, We granted to Mūsā (Moses) and Hārūn (Aaron) the criterion (of right and wrong), and a shining light [i.e. the Tawrāh (Torah)] and a Reminder for *al-Muttaqūn* (the pious)."** [Sūrah al-Anbiyā' 21:48]

✪ BENEFIT 73

Taqwā is from the reasons for safety on the Day of Standing.

Allāh (سُبْحَانَهُ وَتَعَالَىٰ) said:

﴿ٱتَّقُوا۟ رَبَّكُمْ ۚ إِنَّ زَلْزَلَةَ ٱلسَّاعَةِ شَىْءٌ عَظِيمٌ ﴿١﴾﴾

> **"Fear your Lord and be dutiful to Him! Verily, the earthquake of the Hour (of Judgement) is a terrible thing."** [Sūrah al-Ḥajj 22:1]

✿ BENEFIT 74

Taqwā is from the means of magnifying Allāh's signs.

Allāh (سُبْحَانَهُ وَتَعَالَى) said:

﴿ذَٰلِكَ ۖ وَمَن يُعَظِّمْ شَعَٰٓئِرَ ٱللَّهِ فَإِنَّهَا مِن تَقْوَى ٱلْقُلُوبِ ۝٣٢﴾

> **"Thus, it is an obligation that mankind owes to Allāh and whosoever honors the Symbols of Allāh, then it is truly from the piety of the heart."** [Sūrah al-Ḥajj 22:32]

✿ BENEFIT 75

It is that which connects one to Allāh. Thus, the servant takes benefit. Allāh (سُبْحَانَهُ وَتَعَالَى) said:

﴿وَلَٰكِن يَنَالُهُ ٱلتَّقْوَىٰ مِنكُمْ﴾

> **"It is piety from you that reaches Him."** [Al-Sūrah al-Ḥajj 22:37]

✿ BENEFIT 76

It is a reason to be admonished by the Qur'ān and other than the Qur'ān. Allāh (سُبْحَانَهُ وَتَعَالَىٰ) said:

﴿وَمَثَلًا مِّنَ ٱلَّذِينَ خَلَوْا۟ مِن قَبْلِكُمْ وَمَوْعِظَةً لِّلْمُتَّقِينَ ﴿٣٤﴾﴾

> **"And the example of those who passed away before you, and an admonition for those who are *al-Muttaqūn*."** [Sūrah an-Nūr 24:34]

✿ BENEFIT 77

It is from the means of success, the obtainment of what is requested, and the safety of what is feared.

Allāh the Most High said:

﴿وَمَن يُطِعِ ٱللَّهَ وَرَسُولَهُۥ وَيَخْشَ ٱللَّهَ وَيَتَّقْهِ فَأُو۟لَٰٓئِكَ هُمُ ٱلْفَآئِزُونَ ﴿٥٢﴾﴾

> **"And whosoever obeys Allāh and His Messenger (صَلَّى ٱللَّهُ عَلَيْهِ وَسَلَّمَ), fears Allāh, and keeps his duty (to Him), such are the successful ones."** [An-Sūrah an-Nūr 24:52]

✪ BENEFIT 78

Those characterized with *Taqwā* are promised the *Jannah* Allāh the Most High said:

﴿أَذَٰلِكَ خَيۡرٌ أَمۡ جَنَّةُ ٱلۡخُلۡدِ ٱلَّتِي وُعِدَ ٱلۡمُتَّقُونَ﴾

> **"Is that (torment) better or the Paradise of Eternity promised to the *Muttaqūn*?"** [Sūrah al-Furqān 25:15]

✪ BENEFIT 79

The *Muttaqīn* have whatever they want in the *Jannah*.

Allāh (سُبْحَانَهُ وَتَعَالَىٰ) said:

﴿لَّهُمۡ فِيهَا مَا يَشَآءُونَ خَٰلِدِينَ﴾

> **"For them, there will be therein all that they desire, and they will abide (there forever)."** [Sūrah al-Furqān 25:16]

✪ BENEFIT 80

The *Jannah* is brought near to those characterized by *Taqwā*.

Allāh (سُبْحَانَهُ وَتَعَالَىٰ) said:

﴿وَأُزْلِفَتِ ٱلْجَنَّةُ لِلْمُتَّقِينَ ۝٩٠﴾

"And Paradise will be brought near to the *Muttaqūn*."
[Sūrah ash-Shuʿarāʾ 26:90]

✿ BENEFIT 81

Taqwā is from the reasons of safety from punishment in this world. Allāh (سُبْحَانَهُ وَتَعَالَىٰ) said:

﴿وَأَنجَيْنَا ٱلَّذِينَ ءَامَنُوا۟ وَكَانُوا۟ يَتَّقُونَ ۝٥٣﴾

"And We saved those who believed, and used to fear Allāh, and keep their duty to Him." [Sūrah an-Naml 27:53]

✿ BENEFIT 82

That the praiseworthy outcome is for the *Muttaqīn*.

Allāh (سُبْحَانَهُ وَتَعَالَىٰ) said:

﴿وَٱلْعَـٰقِبَةُ لِلْمُتَّقِينَ ۝٨٣﴾

> **"And the good end is for the *Muttaqūn*."** [Sūrah al-Qaṣaṣ 28:83]

✿ BENEFIT 83

It is from the reasons for the rectification of actions and the forgiveness of sins. Allāh (سُبْحَانَهُ وَتَعَالَىٰ) said:

﴿وَقُولُوا۟ قَوْلًا سَدِيدًا ﴿٧٠﴾ يُصْلِحْ لَكُمْ أَعْمَٰلَكُمْ وَيَغْفِرْ لَكُمْ ذُنُوبَكُمْ﴾

> **"Say a statement that is *Sadīd* (truthful and on point). He will direct you to do righteous good deeds and will forgive you your sins".** [Sūrah al-Aḥzāb 33:70-71]

✿ BENEFIT 84

Taqwā is from the reasons of Mercy.

Allāh (سُبْحَانَهُ وَتَعَالَىٰ) said:

﴿ٱتَّقُوا۟ مَا بَيْنَ أَيْدِيكُمْ وَمَا خَلْفَكُمْ لَعَلَّكُمْ تُرْحَمُونَ ﴿٤٥﴾﴾

> **"Beware of that which is before you (worldly torments), and that which is behind you (torments in the Hereafter), in order that you may receive Mercy (i.e. if you believe in Allāh's Religion Islāmic Monotheism, and avoid polythe-**

> **ism, and obey Allāh with righteous deeds).”** [Sūrah Yā-Sīn 36:45]

✪ BENEFIT 85

It is the elevation of the circumstance of those characterized by *Taqwā*. Allāh (سُبْحَانَهُ وَتَعَالَىٰ) said:

﴿أَمْ نَجْعَلُ ٱلْمُتَّقِينَ كَٱلْفُجَّارِ ٢٨﴾

> **“Or shall We treat the *Muttaqūn* as the *Fujjār* (criminals, disbelievers, wicked, etc.)?”** [Sūrah Sād 38:28]

✪ BENEFIT 86

The good place of return is for the *Muttaqīn*. Allāh (سُبْحَانَهُ وَتَعَالَىٰ) said:

﴿وَإِنَّ لِلْمُتَّقِينَ لَحُسْنَ مَـَٔابٍ ٤٩﴾

> **“Verily, for the *Muttaqūn* is a good final return (Paradise)”** [Sūrah Sād 38:49]

✿ BENEFIT 87

The results of *Taqwā* are truthfulness and attestation Allāh the Most High said:

﴿وَٱلَّذِى جَآءَ بِٱلصِّدْقِ وَصَدَّقَ بِهِۦٓ أُو۟لَـٰٓئِكَ هُمُ ٱلْمُتَّقُونَ ۝٣٣﴾

> **"And he (Muḥammad ﷺ) who has brought the truth (this Qur'ān and Islāmic Monotheism) and (those who) believed therein (i.e. the true believers of Islāmic Monotheism), those are *al-Muttaqūn*."** [Sūrah az-Zumar 36:33]

✿ BENEFIT 88

Those characterized with it have whatever they want. Allāh the most high said:

﴿لَهُم مَّا يَشَآءُونَ عِندَ رَبِّهِمْ﴾

> **"They shall have all that they will desire with their Lord. That is the reward of *Muhsinūn* (good doers)."** [Sūrah az-Zumar 36:34]

✪ BENEFIT 89

Taqwā is a reason for the removal of sins and a good reward.

Allāh the most high said:

﴿لِيُكَفِّرَ ٱللَّهُ عَنْهُمْ أَسْوَأَ ٱلَّذِى عَمِلُوا۟ وَيَجْزِيَهُمْ أَجْرَهُم بِأَحْسَنِ
ٱلَّذِى كَانُوا۟ يَعْمَلُونَ ٣٥﴾

> **"So that Allāh may remit from them the evil of what they did and give them the reward, according to the best of what they used to do."** [Sūrah az-Zumar 36:35]

✪ BENEFIT 90

Those characterized with it are raised above gardens along with complete bliss.

Allāh the Most High said:

﴿لَٰكِنِ ٱلَّذِينَ ٱتَّقَوْا۟ رَبَّهُمْ لَهُمْ غُرَفٌ مِّن فَوْقِهَا غُرَفٌ مَّبْنِيَّةٌ تَجْرِى مِن تَحْتِهَا ٱلْأَنْهَٰرُ﴾

> **"But those who fear Allāh and keep their duty to their Lord (Allāh), for them are built lofty rooms; one above another under which rivers flow (i.e. Paradise)."** [Sūrah az-Zumar 36:20]

✪ BENEFIT 91

It is from the reasons of being safe from dangerous situations and having security from evil.

Allāh the Most High said:

﴿وَيُنَجِّي ٱللَّهُ ٱلَّذِينَ ٱتَّقَوْاْ بِمَفَازَتِهِمْ لَا يَمَسُّهُمُ ٱلسُّوٓءُ وَلَا هُمْ يَحْزَنُونَ ﴿٦١﴾﴾

> **"And Allāh will deliver those who are the *Muttaqūn* (the pious) to their places of success (Paradise). Evil shall touch them not, nor shall they grieve."** [Sūrah az-Zumar 36:61]

✪ BENEFIT 92

The *Muttaqīn* will be carried to the *Jannah* in groups in a manner of nobility and immortality Allāh (سُبْحَانَهُ وَتَعَالَىٰ) said:

﴿وَسِيقَ ٱلَّذِينَ ٱتَّقَوْاْ رَبَّهُمْ إِلَى ٱلْجَنَّةِ زُمَرًا ۖ حَتَّىٰٓ إِذَا جَآءُوهَا
وَفُتِحَتْ أَبْوَٰبُهَا وَقَالَ لَهُمْ خَزَنَتُهَا سَلَٰمٌ عَلَيْكُمْ طِبْتُمْ فَٱدْخُلُوهَا
خَٰلِدِينَ ﴿٧٣﴾ وَقَالُواْ ٱلْحَمْدُ لِلَّهِ ٱلَّذِى صَدَقَنَا وَعْدَهُۥ وَأَوْرَثَنَا
ٱلْأَرْضَ نَتَبَوَّأُ مِنَ ٱلْجَنَّةِ حَيْثُ نَشَآءُ ۖ فَنِعْمَ أَجْرُ ٱلْعَٰمِلِينَ ﴿٧٤﴾﴾

> **"And those who kept their duty to their Lord will be led to Paradise in groups, till, when they reach it, and its gates will be opened (before their arrival for their recep-**

tion) and its keepers will say: *Salāmun 'Alaikum* (peace be upon you)! You have done well, so enter here to abide therein. And they will say: All the praises and thanks be to Allāh Who has fulfilled His Promise to us and has made us inherit (this) land. We can dwell in Paradise where we will; how excellent a reward for the (pious good) workers!" [Sūrah az-Zumar 36:73-74]

✪ BENEFIT 93

Taqwā is from the means of having safety from the punishment in this life. Allāh (سُبْحَانَهُ وَتَعَالَىٰ) said:

﴿وَنَجَّيْنَا ٱلَّذِينَ ءَامَنُوا۟ وَكَانُوا۟ يَتَّقُونَ ١٨﴾

"We saved those who believed and used to fear Allāh, keep their duty to Him and avoid evil." [Sūrah Fuṣṣilat 41:18]

✪ BENEFIT 94

that the hereafter is for those characterized with *Taqwā* Allāh (سُبْحَانَهُ وَتَعَالَىٰ) said:

﴿وَٱلْـَٔاخِرَةُ عِندَ رَبِّكَ لِلْمُتَّقِينَ ٣٥﴾

"The Hereafter with your Lord is only for the *Muttaqūn*." [Sūrah az-Zukhruf 43:35]

✪ BENEFIT 95

friendship between the loved ones with *Taqwā* is established in this world as well as the hereafter.

Allāh (سُبْحَانَهُ وَتَعَالَىٰ) said:

﴿ٱلْأَخِلَّآءُ يَوْمَئِذٍۭ بَعْضُهُمْ لِبَعْضٍ عَدُوٌّ إِلَّا ٱلْمُتَّقِينَ ٦٧﴾

> **"Friends on that Day will be foes one to another except *al-Muttaqūn*."** [Sūrah az-Zukhruf 43:67]

✪ BENEFIT 96

The station of those characterized with *Taqwā* is a place of safety in gardens and springs with what is in it, of bliss. Allāh (سُبْحَانَهُ وَتَعَالَىٰ) said:

﴿إِنَّ ٱلْمُتَّقِينَ فِى مَقَامٍ أَمِينٍ ٥١ فِى جَنَّٰتٍ وَعُيُونٍ ٥٢ يَلْبَسُونَ مِن سُندُسٍ وَإِسْتَبْرَقٍ مُّتَقَٰبِلِينَ ٥٣ كَذَٰلِكَ وَزَوَّجْنَٰهُم بِحُورٍ عِينٍ ٥٤ يَدْعُونَ فِيهَا بِكُلِّ فَٰكِهَةٍ ءَامِنِينَ ٥٥ لَا يَذُوقُونَ فِيهَا ٱلْمَوْتَ إِلَّا ٱلْمَوْتَةَ ٱلْأُولَىٰ ۖ وَوَقَىٰهُمْ عَذَابَ ٱلْجَحِيمِ ٥٦ فَضْلًا مِّن رَّبِّكَ ۚ ذَٰلِكَ هُوَ ٱلْفَوْزُ ٱلْعَظِيمُ ٥٧﴾

> **"Verily, the *Muttaqūn* (the pious), will be in place of Security (Paradise). Among Gardens and Springs, dressed in**

fine silk and (also) in thick silk, facing each other, so (it will be). And We shall marry them to *Hūr* (fair female) with wide, lovely eyes. They will call therein for every kind of fruit in peace and security they will never taste death therein except the first death (of this world), and He will save them from the torment of the blazing Fire, as a Bounty from your Lord! That will be the supreme success!" [Sūrah ad-Dukhān 44:51-57]

✪ BENEFIT 97

Taqwā is from the means of Allāh's protection Allāh (سُبۡحَانَهُۥ وَتَعَالَىٰ) said:

﴿وَٱللَّهُ وَلِيُّ ٱلۡمُتَّقِينَ ١٩﴾

"Allāh is the *Walī* (Helper, Protector) of the *Muttaqūn*." [Sūrah al-Jāthiyah 45:19]

✪ BENEFIT 98

Those characterized with *Taqwā* have been promised, the *Jannah* which has various forms of bliss within it.

Allāh (سُبۡحَانَهُۥ وَتَعَالَىٰ) said:

﴿مَّثَلُ ٱلۡجَنَّةِ ٱلَّتِي وُعِدَ ٱلۡمُتَّقُونَۖ فِيهَآ أَنۡهَٰرٞ مِّن مَّآءٍ غَيۡرِ ءَاسِنٖ وَأَنۡهَٰرٞ

مِّن لَّبَنٍ لَّمْ يَتَغَيَّرْ طَعْمُهُۥ وَأَنْهَـٰرٌ مِّنْ خَمْرٍ لَّذَّةٍ لِّلشَّـٰرِبِينَ وَأَنْهَـٰرٌ مِّنْ عَسَلٍ
مُّصَفًّى ۖ وَلَهُمْ فِيهَا مِن كُلِّ ٱلثَّمَرَٰتِ وَمَغْفِرَةٌ مِّن رَّبِّهِمْ ۖ كَمَنْ هُوَ خَـٰلِدٌ فِى
ٱلنَّارِ وَسُقُوا۟ مَآءً حَمِيمًا فَقَطَّعَ أَمْعَآءَهُمْ ﴿١٥﴾

"The description of Paradise which the *Muttaqūn* (the pious) have been promised (is that) in it are rivers of water the taste and smell of which are not changed, rivers of milk of which the taste never changes, rivers of wine delicious to those who drink, and rivers of clarified honey (clear and pure) therein for them is every kind of fruit, and forgiveness from their Lord. (Are these) like those who shall dwell forever in the Fire and be given to drink boiling water so that it cuts up their bowels?" [Sūrah Muḥammad 47:15]

✪ BENEFIT 99

Taqwā is from the means of obtaining reward.

Allāh (سُبْحَانَهُ وَتَعَالَىٰ) said:

﴿وَإِن تُؤْمِنُوا۟ وَتَتَّقُوا۟ يُؤْتِكُمْ أُجُورَكُمْ﴾

"If you believe (in the Oneness of Allāh - Islāmic Monotheism), and fear Allāh, and avoid evil, He will grant you your wages." [Sūrah Muḥammad 47:36]

✪ BENEFIT 100

Taqwā is a means for mercy. Allāh (سُبْحَانَهُ وَتَعَالَىٰ) said:

﴿وَاتَّقُوا اللَّهَ لَعَلَّكُمْ تُرْحَمُونَ ١٠﴾

> **"Fear Allāh, that you may receive mercy."** [Sūrah al-Ḥujurāt 49:10]

✪ BENEFIT 101

By way of *Taqwā* nobility with Allāh is obtained. Allāh (سُبْحَانَهُ وَتَعَالَىٰ) said:

﴿إِنَّ أَكْرَمَكُمْ عِندَ اللَّهِ أَتْقَاكُمْ﴾

> **"Verily, the most honorable of you with Allāh is that (believer) who has *at-Taqwā*."** [Sūrah al-Ḥujurāt 49:13]

✪ BENEFIT 102

Taqwā is from the means of magnifying the messenger of Allāh (صَلَّى اللَّهُ عَلَيْهِ وَسَلَّمَ). Allāh (سُبْحَانَهُ وَتَعَالَىٰ) said:

﴿إِنَّ الَّذِينَ يَغُضُّونَ أَصْوَاتَهُمْ عِندَ رَسُولِ اللَّهِ أُولَٰئِكَ

﴿ ٱلَّذِينَ ٱمۡتَحَنَ ٱللَّهُ قُلُوبَهُمۡ لِلتَّقۡوَىٰ ﴾

"Verily, those who lower their voices in the presence of Allāh's Messenger (صَلَّىٰ ٱللَّهُ عَلَيْهِ وَسَلَّمَ), they are the ones whose hearts Allāh has tested for piety." [Sūrah al-Ḥujurāt 49:3]

✪ BENEFIT 103

The *Jannah* is brought near for those characterized with *Taqwā*.

Allāh (سُبْحَانَهُ وَتَعَالَىٰ) said:

﴿ وَأُزۡلِفَتِ ٱلۡجَنَّةُ لِلۡمُتَّقِينَ غَيۡرَ بَعِيدٍ ٣١ ﴾

"And Paradise will be brought near to the *Muttaqūn*, not far off." [Sūrah Qāf 50:31]

✪ BENEFIT 104

The reward of those characterized with *Taqwā* are gardens Allāh (سُبْحَانَهُ وَتَعَالَىٰ) said:

﴿ إِنَّ ٱلۡمُتَّقِينَ فِي جَنَّٰتٖ وَعُيُونٍ ١٥ ﴾

"Verily, the *Muttaqūn* (the pious) will be in the midst of

> **Gardens and Springs (in the Paradise).”** [Sūrah adh-Dhāriyāt 51:15]

✪ BENEFIT 105

That the reward of those characterized with *Taqwā* are gardens.

Allāh (سُبْحَانَهُ وَتَعَالَىٰ) said:

﴿إِنَّ ٱلْمُتَّقِينَ فِى جَنَّٰتٍ وَنَعِيمٍ ١٧﴾

> **“Verily, the *Muttaqūn* (the pious) will be in Gardens (Paradise), and Delight.”** [Sūrah at-Ṭūr 52:17]

✪ BENEFIT 106

That *Taqwā* inherits the *Khashyah* of Allāh. Allāh (سُبْحَانَهُ وَتَعَالَىٰ) said:

﴿قَالُوٓا۟ إِنَّا كُنَّا قَبْلُ فِىٓ أَهْلِنَا مُشْفِقِينَ ٢٦﴾

> **“Saying: ‘Aforetime, we were afraid (of the punishment of Allāh) in the midst of our families.’”** [Sūrah at-Ṭūr 52:26]

✪ BENEFIT 107

The reward of those characterized with *Taqwā* are Gardens and their bliss Allāh (سُبْحَانَهُ وَتَعَالَىٰ) said:

﴿إِنَّ ٱلْمُتَّقِينَ فِى جَنَّٰتٍ وَنَهَرٍ ۝٥٤﴾

> **"Verily, the *Muttaqūn*, will be in the midst of Gardens and Rivers (Paradise)."** [Sūrah al-Qamar54:54]

✪ BENEFIT 108

Taqwā is from the means of having mercy, guidance and forgiveness compounded Allāh (سُبْحَانَهُ وَتَعَالَىٰ) said:

﴿يَٰٓأَيُّهَا ٱلَّذِينَ ءَامَنُوا۟ ٱتَّقُوا۟ ٱللَّهَ وَءَامِنُوا۟ بِرَسُولِهِۦ يُؤْتِكُمْ
كِفْلَيْنِ مِن رَّحْمَتِهِۦ وَيَجْعَل لَّكُمْ نُورًا تَمْشُونَ بِهِۦ وَيَغْفِرْ لَكُمْ﴾

> **"O you who believe [in Mūsā (Moses) (i.e. Jews) and 'Īsā (Jesus) (i.e. Christians)]! Fear Allāh and believe in His Messenger (Muḥammad صَلَّى ٱللَّهُ عَلَيْهِ وَسَلَّمَ), He will give you a double portion of His Mercy, and He will give you a light by which you shall walk (straight). And He will forgive you."** [Sūrah al-Ḥadīd 57:28]

✿ BENEFIT 109

Taqwā is a reason to be removed from matters of constraint and have plentiful provisions Allāh (سُبْحَانَهُ وَتَعَالَىٰ) said:

﴿وَمَن يَتَّقِ ٱللَّهَ يَجْعَل لَّهُۥ مَخْرَجًا ۝٢ وَيَرْزُقْهُ مِنْ حَيْثُ لَا يَحْتَسِبُ﴾

> **"And whosoever fears Allāh and keeps his duty to Him, He will make a way for him to get out (from every difficulty). And He will provide him from (sources) he never could imagine."** [Sūrah at-Ṭalāq 65:2-3]

✿ BENEFIT 110

Taqwā is a means for the ease of matters. Allāh (سُبْحَانَهُ وَتَعَالَىٰ) said:

﴿وَمَن يَتَّقِ ٱللَّهَ يَجْعَل لَّهُۥ مِنْ أَمْرِهِۦ يُسْرًا ۝٤﴾

> **"Whosoever fears Allāh and keeps his duty to Him, He will make his matter easy for him."** [Sūrah at-Ṭalāq 65:4]

✿ BENEFIT 111

That *Taqwā* is a reason for the removal of sins and the obtainment of much rewards. Allāh (سُبْحَانَهُ وَتَعَالَىٰ) said:

﴿وَمَن يَتَّقِ ٱللَّهَ يُكَفِّرۡ عَنۡهُ سَيِّـَٔاتِهِۦ وَيُعۡظِمۡ لَهُۥٓ أَجۡرًا ۝٥﴾

"Whosoever fears Allāh and keeps his duty to Him, He will expiate from him his sins, and will enlarge his reward." [Sūrah at-Ṭalāq 65:5]

BENEFIT 112

The reward of those characterized with *Taqwā* is gardens. Allāh (سُبْحَانَهُ وَتَعَالَىٰ) said:

﴿إِنَّ لِلۡمُتَّقِينَ عِندَ رَبِّهِمۡ جَنَّٰتِ ٱلنَّعِيمِ ۝٣٤﴾

"Verily, for the *Muttaqūn* are Gardens of delight (Paradise) with their Lord." [Sūrah al-Qalam 68:34]

BENEFIT 113

Those characterized with *Taqwā* are those who take reminder by the Qur'ān Allāh (سُبْحَانَهُ وَتَعَالَىٰ) said:

﴿وَإِنَّهُۥ لَتَذۡكِرَةٞ لِّلۡمُتَّقِينَ ۝٤٨﴾

"And verily, this (Qur'ān) is a Reminder for the *Muttaqūn*." [Sūrah al-Ḥāqqah 69:48]

✪ BENEFIT 114

The reward of the *Muttaqīn* are shades, springs and fruits from that which they desire. Allāh (سُبْحَانَهُ وَتَعَالَىٰ) said:

﴿إِنَّ ٱلْمُتَّقِينَ فِي ظِلَٰلٍ وَعُيُونٍ ۝٤١ وَفَوَٰكِهَ مِمَّا يَشْتَهُونَ ۝٤٢﴾

> **"Verily, the *Muttaqūn* shall be amidst shades and springs."**
> [Sūrah al-Mursalāt 77:41-42]

✪ BENEFIT 115

The reward of those characterized with *Taqwā* is success with bliss Allāh (سُبْحَانَهُ وَتَعَالَىٰ) said:

﴿إِنَّ لِلْمُتَّقِينَ مَفَازًا ۝٣١ حَدَآئِقَ وَأَعْنَٰبًا ۝٣٢ وَكَوَاعِبَ أَتْرَابًا ۝٣٣ وَكَأْسًا دِهَاقًا ۝٣٤
لَّا يَسْمَعُونَ فِيهَا لَغْوًا وَلَا كِذَّٰبًا ۝٣٥ جَزَآءً مِّن رَّبِّكَ عَطَآءً حِسَابًا ۝٣٦﴾

> **"Verily, for the *Muttaqūn*, there will be a success (Paradise); Gardens and vineyards, And young full-breasted (mature) maidens of equal age, and a full cup (of wine). No *Laghw* (dirty, false, evil talk) shall they hear therein, nor lying; A reward from your Lord, an ample calculated gift (according to the best of their good deeds)."**
> [Sūrah an-Nabā' 78:31-36]

BENEFIT 116

Taqwā is from the reasons for the facilitation of that which is easy. Allāh (سُبْحَانَهُ وَتَعَالَىٰ) said:

﴿فَأَمَّا مَنْ أَعْطَىٰ وَٱتَّقَىٰ ۝٥ وَصَدَّقَ بِٱلْحُسْنَىٰ ۝٦ فَسَنُيَسِّرُهُۥ لِلْيُسْرَىٰ ۝٧﴾

> **"As for him who gives (in charity) and keeps his duty to Allāh, fears Him, and believes in *al-Husnā*. We will make smooth for him the path of ease (goodness)."** [Sūrah al-Layl 92:5-7]

✪ BENEFIT 117

It is a reason for safety from the hellfire. Allāh (سُبْحَانَهُ وَتَعَالَىٰ) said:

﴿وَسَيُجَنَّبُهَا ٱلْأَتْقَى ۝١٧ ٱلَّذِى يُؤْتِى مَالَهُۥ يَتَزَكَّىٰ ۝١٨ وَمَا لِأَحَدٍ عِندَهُۥ مِن نِّعْمَةٍ تُجْزَىٰٓ ۝١٩ إِلَّا ٱبْتِغَآءَ وَجْهِ رَبِّهِ ٱلْأَعْلَىٰ ۝٢٠ وَلَسَوْفَ يَرْضَىٰ ۝٢١﴾

> **"And *al-Muttaqūn* (the pious) will be far removed from it (Hell). He who spends his wealth for increase in self-purification, and who has (in mind) no favor from anyone to be paid back, except to seek the Countenance of his Lord, the Most-High. He, surely, will be pleased (when he enters Paradise)."** [Sūrah al-Layl 92:17-21]

And with this the benefits of *Taqwā* that have been mentioned in the

Noble Qur'ān in accordance to what we have followed up, they have reached 64 benefits of those things that have not been reiterated and of the matters that have been reiterated have reached 107 benefits.

Conclusion

All praise is due to Allāh, the Lord of everything in existence who by way of his blessings the righteous matters are completed and the one who bestows upon whoever he wants from His servants and guides them to the truth, and he has led many astray from the truth due to a wisdom that he wants. So, glory be to *al-Ḥakīm*, *al-ʿAlīm*, *al-Birr*, *ar-Raḥīm*.

Our Lord, bestow upon us from your mercy. Verily, you are *al-Wahhāb*. Oh, Allāh! Make us of those who are characterized with those descriptions so that you will be pleased with them, and they will be pleased with you. Oh, *Ḥayy al-Qayyūm*, Oh, the One Who in whose hand is the dominions of the earth and the heavens! May Allāh mention our Prophet Muḥammad with praise in the highest of gatherings and have peace upon him, upon his family, his companions, and whoever follows them in good with perfection until the Day of Reckoning.